AN ELEMENTARY GEOGRAPHY

OF

INDIA, BURMA, AND CEYLON

AN ELEMENTARY GEOGRAPHY

OF

INDIA, BURMA, AND CEYLON

BY

HENRY F. BLANFORD, F.R.S.

GYAN

Published by

GYAN

Gyan Publishing House
5, Ansari Road
Daryaganj, New Delhi-110002
Phone: 011-47034999, 9811692060
E-mail: books@gyanbooks.com

Distribution Network
gyanbooks.com
India, USA, Canada, UK, Australia

ISBN: 978-81-212-5559-2 (HB)
First Published, 1890

2nd Impression 2024

Printed at: Gyan Press, Delhi.

AN ELEMENTARY GEOGRAPHY OF INDIA, BURMA, AND CEYLON

Author: HENRY F. BLANFORD

AN ELEMENTARY GEOGRAPHY

OF

INDIA, BURMA, AND CEYLON

AN ELEMENTARY GEOGRAPHY

OF

INDIA, BURMA, AND CEYLON

BY

HENRY F. BLANFORD, F.R.S.

LATE METEOROLOGICAL REPORTER TO THE GOVERNMENT OF INDIA

London

MACMILLAN AND CO.

AND NEW YORK

1890

PREFACE

In this little book the geography of the Indian Empire is described on the same general plan as that adopted by Dr. Geikie in his *Geography of the British Isles*, but with such modifications as were found necessary in dealing with a country far more extensive, diversified, and unfamiliar in most of its aspects. In order to bring so large a subject within the modest limits of less than 200 pages, it has been necessary to restrict the description to such features as are most characteristic and important, and it has not been possible to enter into much detail. Teachers and others who may require such for their own information may readily obtain it in Dr. George Smith's excellent *Students' Geography of British India*, in Sir W. W. Hunter's *Indian Empire*, and especially the *Imperial Gazetteer of India*, and the numerous articles in the ninth edition of the *Encyclopædia Britannica*. Elphinstone's *History of India*, edited by Professor E. B. Cowell, is perhaps the best work of reference for the history of the Indian people under their Hindu and Muhammadan rulers, and for the elucidation of such few historic allusions as are to be met with in these pages. And for a philosophical insight into the character and social condition of the people of India, no work can compare with Sir Alfred Lyall's *Asiatic Studies*.

In the course of long service in India the author has had occasion to visit most parts of the Empire, and much of the general description of the country and its provinces is either based on or controlled by the results of personal observation. But of course the great mass of the information has been taken from other authentic sources, and the author is also indebted to several friends for additional information on certain subjects for which his own means of reference were insufficient.

The statistics of areas, population, etc., are given chiefly for comparison, and in order to inculcate true ideas of proportion, not for the purpose of burdening the pupil's mind with tables of unmeaning figures.

The illustrations are for the most part taken from photographs. Many of those of the natives of India have been copied, with the courteous permission of Dr. Rost, the chief librarian of the India Office, from the beautiful series collected by the Government of India. It is due to Messrs. Cooper and Sons, the engravers, to testify to the truthfulness of their reproduction as woodcuts.

In the spelling of Indian names, the authorised lists issued by the Government of India have been followed. The principle on which these lists have been drawn up is that the names of well known places that have acquired a fixed English spelling, such as Calcutta, Delhi, Lucknow, Cawnpore, etc., are written in the usual form. In the case of others, the native spelling is followed more or less closely in so far as the elemental sounds can be represented by English letters. By attention to a few simple rules the proper pronunciation of these names can be easily mastered.

Consonants have the same sound as in English, observing that *g* is always hard as in *gig; ch* has the same sound as in *church;* and *sh* the ordinary English sound as in *shall.* Except after these two letters *h* is always an aspirate, and the consonant that it follows is aspirated.

The accent is thrown on the accented syllable : *á* always has the same sound as in *father* ; *é* that of *a* in *mate* or *ê* in the French *même* ; *í* that of *ee* in *feel* ; *ó* that of *o* in *pole* ; and *ú* that of *u* in *rule* or *oo* in *pool*.

The unaccented *a* has generally the sound of *u* in *but*, or better, that of the *o* in *button* ; *e* that of *e* in *met* or of the French *é* in *été* ; *i* that of *i* in *fill* ; *o* that of *o* in *folly* ; and *u* its sound in *put*.

These rules of course do not apply to Anglicised names, nor do they to those of most places in Burma, but Indian names of objects and technical terms, such as *pipal*, *pandit*, *rath*, *vihára*, *Khádar*, etc., are spelt and should be pronounced according to the same system. It is to be regretted, perhaps, that the system of accenting the long vowels has not been quite rigorously adhered to, since the *u* in the final syllable *pur* (*púr*, a town), so common in Indian names, though unaccented is a long vowel, and the first A in Aligarh is long, but not the second. In a few instances, also, the official lists are discordant in the different provinces. Thus the rivers Són, Gandak, Mahánadi, etc., of the Central Provinces and the North-West Provinces appear as the Soane, Gunduk, Mahanuddy, etc., in the Bengal list. In such cases both forms are given in these pages.

CONTENTS

LIST OF ILLUSTRATIONS

THE INDIAN EMPIRE

We speak of India as of a single country, because it is under one supreme government; but it is really a collection of many countries, differing from each other in soil, climate, and productions, in the races that occupy them, in the languages, religions, and civilisation of their peoples, and in many other respects. Yet no country is more distinctly marked off by natural boundaries. Although it forms a part of Asia it is nearly cut off from the remainder of the continent by the great mountain chain, the Himalaya, on its northern border, and the almost equally lofty, cold, and barren table-land of Tibet beyond; while its southern half projects into the Indian Ocean, and is bounded on both sides by the sea. On the north-east and north-west also it is enclosed by mountains, but these are less lofty than the Himalaya, and the countries beyond them are not so high and barren as Tibet. From both these quarters immigrants and invaders in past times have penetrated to India, and especially from the north-west, the frontier of Afghánistán and Balúchistán. But India is most accessible from the sea; and for centuries past, and more than ever at the present day, it has communicated with other countries chiefly from its coasts.

Influence of India's Geography on its People.—Owing to the fertility of its soil and the industry of its inhabitants, it is one of the most productive countries in the world, and, on the whole, one of the most densely peopled; from very early times it has carried on an important commerce, exchanging its natural products and manufactures for those of other countries. In this respect it resembles Britain. But whereas the foreign sea-trade of Britain has been founded and carried on by the inhabitants of the country itself, that of India has been left almost entirely in the hands of foreign sailors; formerly the Arabs and Greeks, and now those of the whole civilised world, especially the British.

The explanation of these and many other important facts in the present condition and past history of the people of India is to be found, partly, at least, in the geography of the country. That India is so richly productive is owing to the vast extent of its fertile plains, and to its climate, which is one of the warmest on the earth's surface, while most parts receive a sufficient and some a very abundant rainfall; this combination of circumstances being that which makes agriculture easy and very profitable. And this productiveness, on the one hand, has attracted immigrants and invaders from the poorer countries beyond its frontier, and on the other hand, has fostered trade, which consists in different countries or provinces exchanging with each other so much of their productions as are not required for the consumption of their own inhabitants. Hence the inhabitants of the towns and cities of India have long been keen traders, carrying on an active inland trade between the different provinces. How is it, then, that India has produced no race of sailors, like the Arabs, to carry her superfluous produce to distant countries?[1]

The answer to this question will probably be that the Hindu religion discourages travelling by sea. And this is no doubt true, but the explanation is far from complete.

[1] It must not be understood from these remarks that there are no Indian sailors, nor that in past times the Hindus have always abstained from sea travel. At present indeed the Indian seafaring population (fishermen and boatmen excepted) is almost entirely Muhammadan; but centuries before the advent of Muhammadans, there was an active coasting trade as at present, which must have been carried on by Hindus; and the conquest of Ceylon by Wijáyo from Bengal, and the colonisation of Pegu and Java by Telingas, from the shores of the Godávari delta, show that the Hindus must have had considerable intercourse with these countries many centuries before the Christian era. The statement in the text is, however, not invalidated by these facts.

It is generally found that customs that have been sanctioned by the popular religion, and seem to have been imposed by it, have really been brought about by other causes; either by something that has happened in the past history of the people, or, more often, by something or other in the circumstances of their country. And such is probably the case here. In the first place, a country that produces in profusion all that is necessary to its inhabitants, and in addition most of the luxuries of life, offers but little stimulus to sea enterprise. The great seafaring nations of antiquity were not those of such rich countries as the Nile delta, Mesopotamia, or the plains of China; nor in mediæval times the people of Southern France or the plains of Italy; but the Phœnicians, Arabs, Greeks, Scandinavians, and Genoese, all denizens of mountainous or rocky countries, and the Venetians, whose original possessions were restricted to a few marshy islands. And in the second place, while the irregular coasts of such countries as Greece, Norway, and Britain abound in landlocked nooks and harbours where the seagoing craft can lie up in safety, it needs but a glance at the map of India, at the straight unbroken coast-lines of the peninsula, to show us how deficient that coast is in this respect. There is not a single good harbour on the whole length of the east coast, and but very few on the west coast south of Bombay; and therefore the first requisite for training a race of sailors, and for building and sheltering sea-going ships, is wanting. It is true that several large rivers discharge their waters on the east coast, and we might perhaps expect that ships would enter these rivers and find protection in their channels, as they do in those of the Ganges and the Irawadi. But this is not so. Strong sea-currents run up or down the coast at different seasons of the year, and have caused all these rivers to form bars[1] across their mouths, rendering the entrance so shallow that only small boats can pass into them, and therefore they are useless as harbours for seagoing ships.

Even more than for its natural productions and costly

[1] See *Physical Geography for Indian Schools*, chap. viii.

manufactures, India was famous in very ancient times as a land of learning and speculative philosophy. It has been usual to attribute this solely to the character of its inhabitants. But we shall see that it was also due in no small degree to its natural productiveness; in other words, to those circumstances of its soil and climate that we have already noticed. In order to develop learning and the arts, in other words civilisation, a people must possess wealth and enjoy leisure. So long as every one is fully employed in procuring food, and in defending himself against enemies, a nation cannot emerge from barbarism. Now the people who founded the Hindu, Jain, and Buddhist religions, and an elaborate system of speculative philosophy, who civilised India, and gained for it the reputation of learning in ancient times, were the fair race known as Aryas, who entered India from the northwest many centuries before the Christian era. Up to that time they appear to have been a simple pastoral race, unacquainted with the art of writing; and it was not until they had been long settled on the rich plains of northern India that they acquired wealth and leisure, and developed that civilisation and learning that afterwards spread through India and made the name of their country famous among distant nations. The ancient civilisations of Egypt, Babylonia, and China, all more or less similar to that of India, took their rise among races of very different origin, but like that of India, on the fertile plains of great rivers.

Thus we see that in many important respects the character of the native inhabitants of India has been greatly influenced by the geography of their country, especially the productiveness of its soil and the warmth and moisture of its climate. We shall presently notice these and other influences more in detail. But we must first draw attention to another circumstance which has greatly affected the fortunes of the people of India, and which may be traced to the same primary cause. The inhabitants of a warm and damp climate, if industrious, may increase rapidly and may become rich and civilised, but they are seldom robust and warlike, while those of colder climates and poorer countries are necessarily more hardy and vigorous, more given to bodily exercise and less weakened by luxurious habits. Hence the very richness and prosperity of the people of India gradually weakened them for purposes of defence, and more particularly those of the dampest and richest provinces ; while they had, and still have on their north-west frontier, in Afghánistán, and in the dry and colder countries of Central Asia, poor, hardy and warlike tribes, to whom the possession or plunder of India has always been a great temptation. The result is shown in the history of the Indian people. In the most remote ages the Aryas, afterwards the Greeks, the Scythians, and in subsequent times the Patháns and the Moguls, have invaded India from this same quarter, and most of them spread over the country, subduing the former inhabitants, and in the end mingling with them, and in their turn yielding to some later invader. None of these invading races ever succeeded in establishing a permanent, stable, and peaceful government throughout the whole extent of the empire. The country was always divided, more or less, into petty states, often at war with each other, and constantly changing their limits ; and thus, for centuries, India has been the battle-ground of contending rulers ; the people were sometimes massacred by invading armies, their towns from time to time besieged and pillaged, their villages and fields laid waste and harried by robber bands, while the roads were often unsafe, and travellers were liable to be robbed and murdered by dacoits (gang-robbers) and Thugs. Now that, for several generations, all India has enjoyed profound peace under a government so strong as to keep out invaders, and to quell those turbulent spirits that would disturb the peace within its own borders, the people have almost forgotten those evil times. But were it not for the strength of the government and its power in organising the people for defence, India would be as open as ever to new invaders and a repetition of all the horrors of former days. Human nature changes but slowly, and in its present prosperous condition, with its large rich cities, and its widely spreading fields, India is more than ever a temptation to the invader. As part of a great nation, the power of which extends to all parts of the world, which can put forth its strength in any quarter that may be threatened with attack, and can bring all the resources of the most advanced civilisation to aid the defence, the people are preserved from these evils, and able to reap in peace the fruits of their industry.

Geographical Position.—The warm climate of India, its damp and rainy summer, the dryness of some provinces

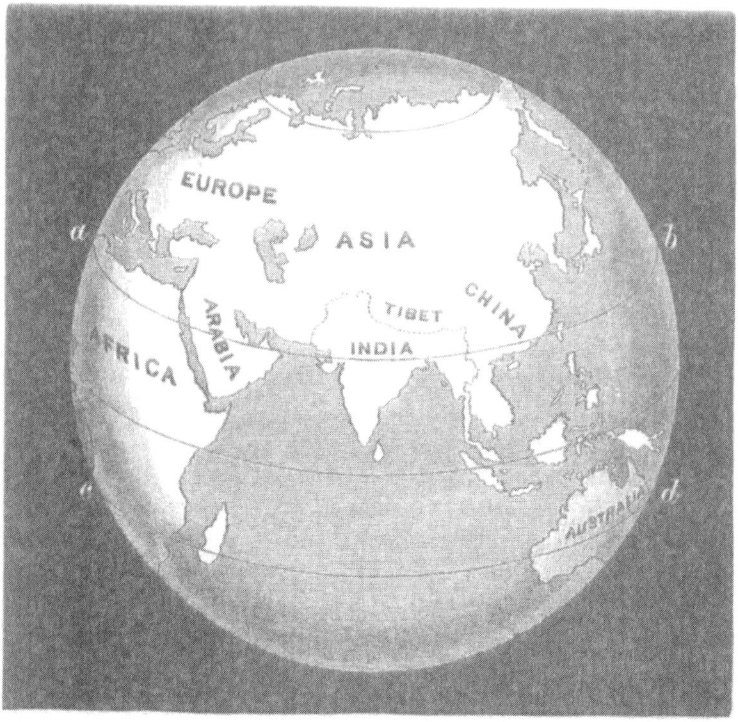

FIG. 1.—POSITION OF INDIA ON THE GLOBE.

and the dampness of others, are due to its geographical position. What this position is will be understood from the accompanying figure (Fig. 1), which represents that half of the globe in which India occupies a central place. The zone included between the two lines *ab* and *cd* (circles on an actual globe) is the tropical zone, the line *ab* which bounds it on the north and runs midway through India being the Tropic of Cancer. This zone is the warmest on the earth's surface. Every place within it has the sun vertically overhead at noon twice in every year, and on the average of the whole year the noonday sun is higher in the heavens than at places outside the Tropics. Now the climate of a place (unless it happens to be high up on a mountain) is the warmer the higher the sun ascends, and since one-half of India lies within the tropical zone, and the remainder only just outside it, India as a whole is a very warm country; the southern half, on the average of the whole year, being warmer than the northern half.

Next notice that it forms a projection, termed a peninsula, on the south of the great continent of Asia. Hence there is land everywhere to the north to a distance of some thousands of miles, while to the south, except the island of Ceylon, is nothing but the ocean. This circumstance, viz. that it is connected with a vast extent of land on the north, and on the south is half surrounded by a sea that forms part of the great ocean, has, as we shall presently see, an important influence on its seasons, especially in producing that strongly marked contrast between the dry and hot season and the rainy season that is so characteristic of India.

Now let us turn to a map of Asia, and we see that though India forms a part of the continent, it is in a great measure isolated from other countries by the lofty table-land of Tibet, of which the Himalaya forms the southern wall. This table-land is so lofty, so mountainous, and so cold and barren, that it can support but few inhabitants, and most of these are wandering tribes that travel from place to place to find pasture for their flocks. It is only in the larger and deeper valleys on its eastern and southern borders that there are any settled inhabitants, and that any cultivation is possible. To reach this table-land from the valley of the Ganges we must first cross the Himalaya, and we should then have to travel due north some 600 miles or more, never descending below 11,000 feet and sometimes ascending to 18,000 feet, or nearly three and a half miles above the sea, before we should reach its northern boundary, and then only to find an arid desert beyond. The Himalaya and Tibet extend far to the east of India, and cut it off completely from the plains of China, while chains of mountains running south from the Himalaya lap round to the east of Assam and Cachar, separating these Indian provinces from Burma and the Chinese province of Yunan.

In the opposite direction, to the north-west, we see that the mountain chain which bears the name of the Himalaya ceases at the Indus; but an extension of the more northern chain of the Tibetan highland, the Mustágh or Kárákoram range, continues under the name of the Hindú Kúsh far beyond that river, and from it other mountains branch off to the south-west through Káfiristán and Afghánistán, and separate these countries and Balúchistán from India. All the country to the west of the Indus consists either of mountains or high plains much intersected with mountains and hills, and the southern part of it is a desert. Access to India from this direction is hardly practicable except along the coast or through Afghánistán and the passes of the western mountains. Beyond Afghánistán, to the west, lies Persia, and to the north, on the farther side of the Hindú Kúsh, Bálkh and Túrkestán, with Búkhára beyond the Oxus river. It was from Afghánistán that came the Greek, Scythian, and Muhammadan invasions of India.

Now let us turn southward and see what countries are India's nearest neighbours across the sea. At the southern extremity of the peninsula, and immediately to the south-east of it, is the island of Lanka or Ceylon. It is separated from India only by a narrow strait of sea, and even this is nearly bridged by the remarkable tongue of land projecting from the coast of Tinnevelly, by Rámeswaram and Manaar islands, together with the shallow reef that links them, and is famous in Hindu legend as Ráma's Bridge. On our modern maps it bears the name of Adam's Bridge. It is really a natural shoal, partly formed by the growth of coral, covered with sand since hardened into stone, and upheaved by natural causes. Ceylon is therefore almost a part of India, and at one time it has doubtless been united to it. But it is noteworthy that some of the common animals of Southern India, and among them the tiger, have never penetrated to Ceylon, so that for long ages past there can have been no complete communication. The people of Ceylon are, however, nearly related to those of India.

If, leaving Madras, we take ship and sail nearly due east across the Bay of Bengal, after a voyage of about 1200 miles we reach the Malay Peninsula, passing between the Andaman and Nicobar islands at rather more than two-thirds of that distance. The Malay Peninsula is a narrow extension of the larger peninsula that encloses the Bay of Bengal on the east, and includes the kingdom of Burma, and beyond it Siam, Tong-King, Annam, Cambodia, and Cochin China. These countries together form the south-eastern portion of Asia. The Malay Peninsula runs farther south than that of India, to within 100 miles of the equator; so that if we are proceeding to China, or even to Siam, we must sail down to its southern extremity, through the narrow sea called the Straits of Malacca which separates the Malay Peninsula from the island of Sumatra. At its southern end is the important British port Singapore, on a little island close to the mainland. Passing this we find ourselves in the China Sea, with the island of Sumatra to the south, and beyond it Java and a great number of smaller islands, most of which belong to the Dutch. On the east is the great island of Borneo, beyond which are Celebes, the Molucca Islands, and New Guinea, and to the north-east of Borneo are the little islands of the Sulu archipelago, and the much larger Philippine Islands belonging to Spain. These islands enclose the China Sea on the east, while its western shores are formed by the Malay Peninsula, Cochin China, Annam, and Tong-King, and its northern shore by China; midway in which is its great southern seaport Canton. And this long sea voyage across the Bay of Bengal, through the Malacca Straits and up the China Sea, is the easiest way of reaching China from India, notwithstanding that on the land side China reaches to the frontier of Upper Burma, and Tibet, which is subject to China, extends along the Himalayan frontier of India; so much easier is it to travel by sea than by land, when there are no railways and no good roads.

Next let us take an imaginary voyage westward. If we

sail from a southern port, say Calicut, and proceed due west, at a distance of 200 miles, or say two days' sailing, we find ourselves among a number of little low islands, none of which rise more than a few feet above the sea surface, and all surrounded by shallow reefs of coral which make navigation dangerous. These are the Lakhadives (100,000 islands). They have been formed entirely by the growth of the coral, which is a kind of animal living only in the sea, where it grows fixed to the bottom like a plant, but it forms a stony skeleton, the remains of which, in the course of ages, accumulate to such an extent as to form groups of islands, such as are the Lakhadives and the Maldives to the south of them. Passing beyond these islands and still sailing westward, we meet with no land for a farther distance of 1100 miles, when we reach the hilly island of Socotra; and if we keep to the north of this island, still on the same course, in about another 200 miles we pass Cape Guardafui, the most easterly point of Africa, and enter the Gulf of Aden, with the shores of Africa on the left and those of Arabia on the right. Finally, after about two days farther voyage up the gulf in a fast steamer, we enter the Red Sea through the Straits of Perim or Bab-el-Mandeb. This is the route to Europe by the Red Sea and the Suez Canal. The steamers from Bombay to Europe take this route, but they pass far to the north of the Lakhadives and generally also of Socotra, so that the first land they meet with after leaving Bombay is the south coast of Arabia.

If, on leaving Bombay, we keep to the north-west, we pass the coasts of Kattywar and Cutch, both portions of India, and reach the port of Kurrachee in Sind beyond the mouths of the Indus; or passing this and sailing westward along the coast of Balúchistán, we enter the Persian Gulf through the Straits of Hormuz, having the coast of Persia on the right and that of Arabia on the left. This is the route to Bushire and Bussora, both at the head of the Persian Gulf, and it was by this route that travellers from Europe frequently reached India in the days when sea navigation was slow and exposed to many dangers.

To the south of India there is no land whatever except

some small coral islands like the Lakhadives; nothing but the broad ocean down to the region of perpetual ice around the Antarctic Pole. But by sailing to the south-west across the Indian Ocean, after many days in a fast steamer or some weeks in a sailing ship, we reach the island of Mauritius, where many natives of India are employed on the sugar plantations, and not a few have settled in trade. Still farther in the same direction, we pass the great island of Madagascar and come to the Cape of Good Hope, which is the most southerly point of Africa. Sailing round this, and then to the north-west across the Atlantic Ocean, was the route always taken by ships between India and Europe for some centuries, before the cutting of the Suez Canal enabled steamers to pass direct from the Red Sea into the Mediterranean; and it is the route still followed by sailing ships, since, although the voyage is much longer, they thus avoid the slow and dangerous navigation of the Red Sea.

Lastly, if we sail to the south-east across the Indian Ocean, after a voyage of at least equal length, we reach the south-west coast of Australia, and if we then proceed due east along this coast, we arrive at the British colonies of Victoria and Tasmania, the latter on a large island near the south-east of Australia; and a few days more in the same direction brings us to New Zealand, also a British colony. This is the route followed by the mail steamers from Bombay to Australia, which take twenty-one days between that port and Melbourne, the capital of Victoria. The Australian colonies may also be reached by another route from India, viz. by way of Singapore; by sailing from the latter port, first to south-east, and then east past Java and through Torres Straits, which separate the most northern point of Australia from New Guinea. After passing these straits, if we follow the Australian coast to the south-east and south, we come successively to the colonies of Queensland and New South Wales on the east coast of Australia, and finally to Victoria on the south-east coast and the island of Tasmania.

Thus we see that although a great number of foreign countries or British possessions are easily reached from India by sea, since lines of steamers or sailing ships run in all the directions we have briefly traced out, none of them are very near India. Indeed, except Ceylon, there is no land of any extent within 1000 miles of Cape Comorin, the nearest being Sumatra, 1250 miles distant. But merchants, sailors and refugees from many distant countries have visited its coasts, and many have settled there and to some extent mingled with the native inhabitants. On the west coast, more particularly, are numerous settlers of foreign origin.

Outer Form, Size, and Boundaries.—It will be seen on the map that the boundaries of India, exclusive of Burma and other British possessions in the eastern peninsula, form an irregular four-sided figure, the longest side being that facing the south-east, and the shortest to the north-west. From the upper end of the Assam valley to Cape Comorin is a distance of nearly 1900 statute miles; from the Yárkand river to Gwádar barely 1100. The Himalayan frontier on the north is about 1600 miles long, measured on a straight line, and the west coast from Gwádar to Cape Comorin 1500 miles. The total area within these limits may be taken in round figures as 1,506,000 square miles. The British possessions in the eastern peninsula, before the annexation of Upper Burma, covered 99,000 square miles, and with this recent addition now amount to 289,000 square miles; so that the total extent of Asiatic country under the supreme government of the Queen-Empress is 1,795,000, or more than one and three-quarter millions of square miles. Of this, however, 738,000 square miles, or about two-fifths, are ruled by Indian native princes, and of the newly annexed territory about one-half consists of tributary states, or is occupied by uncivilised tribes, so that the countries under the immediate administration of British rulers is somewhat less than a million of square miles.

The total area of the British Islands is 121,000 square miles. Therefore that of British India and its dependencies is nearly fifteen times as great, and the portion administered directly by the British Government eight times as great as the native country of its rulers.

Now let us travel round the land frontier of British

India and Burma, and see what is its geographical character, and what states lie around it. Starting from Gwádar Bay in long. 61° 30′ it runs northwards and then eastwards between lat. 30° and 32°, separating Balúchistán from Persia on the west and from Afghánistán on the north. Meeting the Sulemán range to the west of the Indus, it again turns north along this range, to the entrance of the Thal Pass on the Kurram river. Thence it bends eastwards nearly to the Indus, rounding the Afrídi hills. To the north of these it encloses the Pesháwar valley and then runs thirty miles up the course of the Indus. Leaving this river above Amb, it strikes to the north-east along the crest of the range that divides the Indus from its tributary the Siran and farther on from the Kunhar, up to the great peak of Nanga Parbat. From this point it recrosses the Indus, makes a circuit round the lower valley of the Gilgit river, and again continues north-east across the great Mustágh range to the upper valley of the Yárkand river, in lat. 36° 30′, which is the most northerly point of the empire. Following the course of this river to Aktágh, it continues eastward across the Tibetan table-land, including the lofty plain of Lingzi Tang, and separating Kashmir territory from the Chinese province of Káshghár. A little beyond the meridian of 80° E. long. it returns to the south, forming the frontier of Tibet, recrosses the Indus and then the Sutlej at Shipke, and passes through the peak of Gangotri at the head waters of the Ganges. From this peak it follows the Garhwál range south-eastward to the source of the Sárda river, and then striking southwards, follows the course of this stream to the plains. All the mountains for 500 miles to the east of the Sárda are the kingdom of Nepal, and the British boundary runs along or near the foot of the outermost range to about the 88th meridian, when it again makes a circuit northward into the mountains, passing through the great peak of the Kanchinjunga and enclosing the basin of the Teesta, which constitutes the protected state of Sikkim. Beyond this it again follows the foot of the Himalaya (here belonging to Bhotan) to the head of the Assam valley, around which the hills are tenanted by independent tribes. From the head of the Assam valley it runs southwards through the unknown mountains between Assam and Yunan till it crosses the Tapeng river a few miles east of Bhamo, and continues south to the Shwéli river, both tributaries of the Irawadi. Following up the Shwéli to lat. 24°, it winds away eastward across the Mekong or Cambodia river, passing south of Esmok, and probably as far as about the meridian of 103° E. long. About lat. 20° 30′ it returns to the west, till it strikes the Salween river in lat. 20°. All this part of the boundary is at present indeterminate. Yunan lies to the north, Tong-King to the east, and Shan states tributary to Siam to the south. From lat. 20° it follows down the course of the Salween, and then up that of its tributary the Thoung Yin to the crest of the Tenasserim Yoma, the range that divides the drainage of the Gulf of Siam from that of the Bay of Bengal, and finally continues down this range to Point Victoria in lat. 10° N.

Thus we see that the Empire of British India extends from Gwádar Bay on the west, in about E. long. 61° 30′, to the Tong-King frontier on the east, in about E. long. 103°, a range of 41½° of longitude; and from the valley of the Yárkand river on the north, in N. lat. 36° 30′, to Cape Comorin in N. lat. 8°, a range of 28½° of lat. This latter is as great as the distance from the North Cape of Europe to the Pyrenees, and the former, measured on the parallel of 20° as a mean lat., is about 2650 miles, equal to the distance from Valentia on the west coast of Ireland to Astrachan on the Caspian Sea.

General Surface Features.—The surface of India proper, as encircled by the Khirthar and Sulemán ranges bounding the Indus valley on the west, the Himalaya on the north, and the hills of Eastern Bengal and Assam on the east, presents some very conspicuous features, of which we will endeavour to gain a general idea before proceeding to any more detailed description. Immediately within this mountain girdle a broad plain extends from the coast of Sind up the valley of the Indus to the Salt Range, then eastward across the Punjab and down the course of the Jumna and Ganges to the sea-coast of Bengal. Along the centre of this plain one may travel round northern

India from sea to sea without once seeing the smallest hill, and without ever ascending more than 700 feet above the sea-level. This great plain has been formed by the rivers that traverse it; the ground, to a depth of several hundred feet, consisting of layers of sand, clay, and similar materials, brought down by these rivers from the mountains around through long ages, and gradually deposited from their muddy waters. The western half of this plain is little better than desert owing to the want of water, since the rainfall of this part of India is very light and precarious; and indeed all the tract between the Indus and the Arvali range of hills on the east is often spoken of as the great Indian desert. Much of the Western Punjab, except where irrigated from the rivers, is of the same character; but when we turn eastward the rainfall gradually increases, water becomes more abundant, and agriculture more successful, and when we have crossed the Jumna and proceeded some way down the plain traversed by the Ganges, we enter on the richest and most thickly-peopled provinces of India.

Another leading feature of Indian geography is the belt of rugged hilly country that stretches across the peninsula from the Gulf of Cambay almost to the plain of Lower Bengal. This is not a true mountain range like the Himalaya; not a continuous ridge or system of parallel ridges of rocks folded and thrust up above the general level by the same great movement of the earth's crust,[1] but a belt of high land composed of various kinds of rocks that has been less worn down in the course of ages than most of the country to the north and south. On our modern maps the western half of it is called the Sátpura (seven towns) range; the eastern half forms the highlands of Chutia Nágpur. It is probably the same that in ancient times bore the name of the Vindhya range, and was the natural barrier between Hindustán (the country of the Hindus, or Aryan immigrants) on the north and the Deccan (*Dakhin* or South). As Wales was the refuge of the Cymri or ancient inhabitants of Britain when driven from the plains of England by the Saxon invaders, so was

[1] See *Physical Geography for Indian Schools*, chap. iv.

this wild hill tract the refuge of the Gonds and Kóls, the aboriginal people of Central India, when dispossessed in like manner by the invading forefathers of the Hindus on the north, those of the Maráthás on the west, and of the Telugus on the south; and it is the special home of these aboriginal tribes up to the present day. It includes many hills or groups of hills over 3000 and 4000 feet in height; such as the Turan Mal between the Tapti and Nerbudda; the Gawilgarh hills north of Berar; the Pachmarhi or Mahádeva hills near Hoshungábád; the Maikal and Sálétekrí hills, which include the head waters of the Nerbudda, the Són (Soane), and the Mahánadi (Mahánuddy); and Main Pát in Chutia Nágpur.

The Sátpura range is flanked on the north by the valley of the Nerbudda, and on the south by that of the Tapti and its tributary the Púrna, both of which rivers flow through plains many miles across, and 1000 feet or more below the country on each side, and nearly as much above the sea. It is interrupted at one point between Khandwá and the old Mogul city of Burhánpur by a pass or depression in the hills, which affords an easy passage between the two valleys; this has been for centuries the great highway between Northern India and the Deccan, and it is now traversed by the Great Indian Peninsular Railway.

The country north of the Nerbudda up to the Gangetic plain is an undulating table-land, with some hills of no great height. It rises suddenly in an escarpment or steep hill-face immediately to the north of the Nerbudda and Són rivers; that along the Nerbudda called the Vindhya range on our modern maps, and that along the Són the Kaimúr range; and from their crests the general slope of its surface is towards the north, so that all the rivers that carry off its drainage flow northwards into the Jumna and Ganges. On the north-west it graduates into the desert, but on the west it is bounded by the Arvali range, running from Jeypore south-west past Ajmere to Mount Abu. The valley of the Són bounds the table-land on the east, and the country beyond that river, which is equally high, is a broad extension of the highlands of Chutia Nágpur.

The peninsula of India south of the Sátpura and Chutia Nágpur highlands is also in the main a table-land, bounded by a very straight and well-defined escarpment on the west, running parallel with the west coast, and commonly called the Western Ghats, also the Sahyádri range; and on the east by a less definite and continuous escarpment or by lines of hills, which collectively are termed the Eastern Ghats. Like the Sátpuras, these hills are not true mountain ranges, but probably represent ancient coast lines which, except where they have been cut through by the rivers, have been less worn down by the action of the atmosphere and the drainage than other parts of the surface. In general the table-land is highest along its western margin, where in many places it is elevated between 2000 and 3000 feet above the sea; but some other parts are equally high. Thus most of Mysore is over 2000 feet and some parts over 3000 feet. The least-elevated parts are those traversed by the principal rivers, towards which the surface slopes from all directions. Thus Nágpur is but little over 1000 feet; Chándá and Sironchá on the Pénganga and Godávari are but 650 and 400 feet respectively, and Kurnool on the Tungabhadra is not more than 900 feet. This fact that the rivers flow through the lowest parts of the plateau is a general geographical law, and is a consequence of the well-known fact that water always runs towards the lowest level. Another consequence of the same law is that all the great rivers of the peninsula, except the Tapti, which cuts through the Western Ghats, take their rise on the high western margin of the table-land close to the Ghats, and flow eastwards to the Bay of Bengal.

The Eastern and Western Ghats nowhere reach to the present coasts of the peninsula. All round the coast at their foot is a belt of low country between them and the sea. Along the west coast this is narrow, scarcely anywhere more than 50 miles across, and for the most part very hilly; and to the south of the Tapti it is not crossed by any large river, but only by small streams that bring down the drainage of the west face of the Ghats and but very little of that of the table-land beyond their crest;

the only flat low-lying lands fitted for rice cultivation are narrow strips fringing the coast, and along the lower courses of these streams. On the east coast from Ganjam to Cocanada this is equally the case. But south of Cocanada two of the largest rivers of the peninsula enter the sea, and have formed a low flat alluvial plain called a delta [1] with the sand and clay deposited from their waters in the course of ages. Like all river deltas, this is very rich productive land, capable of being irrigated from canals led off from the rivers; and those portions of the Godávari and Kistna districts that include the delta are, next to Tanjore, among the most productive in the peninsula. To the south of Ongole the coast plain is generally wider; only to the north of the Pulicat Lake do the Ghats advance again to within 30 miles of the sea; and from this point they retreat to the south-west till they join the Western Ghats just to the south of the Nilgiri hills, which, near their junction, rise to a height of from 6000 to over 8000 feet. But all the country below and to the south of them is not a plain. About twenty miles to the south of the junction of the Ghats, a range of very lofty hills rises and continues down the remainder of the west coast nearly to Cape Comorin, and several independent groups of hills, from 3000 to 5000 feet high, occupy the central portion of the peninsula down to the valley of the Cauvery. Also the higher parts of the Carnatic lowlands are dotted over with small rocky hills, many of which are crowned with the remains of little hill forts called *Droogs*, the former strongholds of petty chiefs who established themselves in the troublous times that followed on the invasion of the Mogul armies of Aurangzib and the expulsion of the ancient Hindu rulers of the Carnatic. Much of the marginal part of the plain, like that of the Godávari and Kistna districts already mentioned, is flat low-lying land formed by the rivers, and equally fertile. The largest and richest tract of this kind is the district of Tanjore, which is the delta of the Cauvery river.

The surface of the eastern peninsula, or of so much of it as is included in the Indo-British Empire, is of a very different

[1] See *Phys. Geog.*, etc., chap. viii.

character. From the eastern Himalaya, which extends beyond the valley of Assam, several ranges of mountains run out to the south, gradually declining into hills, and the plains between them are comparatively narrow, lying along the courses of the intervening rivers. The only large plain is that of the Irawadi delta. The most westerly of these ranges runs off at the head of the Assam valley, and bears the name of the Pátkai. From this a branch running westwards under the names of the Nágá, Jaintia, Khási, and Gáro hills, separates the Assam valley from that of Cachar and Sylhet. The main range, or rather series of parallel ranges, continues south and runs parallel with the coast of Arakan, separating that province from Ava and Pegu. It becomes lower as it reaches farther south, until at Cape Negrais it sinks into the sea. But even here it does not terminate, but is continued beneath the sea, and its summits reappear here and there above the surface in the chain of islands marked on our maps as Preparis, the Cocos islands, the Andamans, and Nicobars. In Burma it forms the western boundary of the valleys of the Chindwin and the Irawadi. Other ranges divide the Chindwin from the Irawadi, and the two head feeders of the latter river the Mali-Kha from the Meh-Kha, which is probably the same as the Lu-tse-Kiang or Lu river of the Chinese.[1]

Another range again to the east of this last river, and also running south, separates it from the Lan-tsang-Kiang, which in Siam bears the name of the Mekong or Cambodia river. A branch of this last chain continues down the whole length of the Malay Peninsula, terminating at the sea opposite Singapore. Still other ranges occur beyond to the eastward, but these are in China, not in British territory.

Thus a very large proportion of Burma consists of hills, and in the north and also all along the former boundary of British India and Burma these are tenanted for the most part by uncivilised tribes, of whom at present but little is known but their names and their habit of raiding

[1] There is much difference of opinion on the courses of the rivers of Eastern Tibet. The view here adopted is that of General J. T. Walker, the late Surveyor-General of India.

on each other and on the settled inhabitants of the plains, for the purpose of carrying off slaves and the heads of their victims. Farther south, to the east of the Irawadi, the hills are occupied by Shans and Karéns, generally quiet and peaceable people, paying tribute to Burma and now under the protection of the British Government. The Burmese live only in the valleys of the Irawadi and its tributaries.

Climates.—In describing such a country as India we must speak of its climates rather than its climate, so different are its characteristics in the east and the west, and in the extreme north, as compared with its most southerly provinces. Next to the land surface and the character of the soil, perhaps no feature in the geography of a country is so important to its inhabitants as its climate, by which we mean the average character of the weather as hot or cold, dry or moist, at different seasons of the year. It influences their habits of life, their clothing, food, occupations, and the structure of their dwellings. It determines in a large measure whether their lands shall be productive or barren, what kinds of crops they can raise for their food, and whether they can themselves produce the necessaries and luxuries of life or must depend for their supply on other countries. And the character of the people themselves, whether active or inert, is largely controlled by the heat and cold, the dryness or dampness, of the atmosphere in which they live. In India these influences are very apparent. The strongest and most manly races are such as the Patháns, Jats and Rájputs, who inhabit the dry provinces of North-Western India, where the winter is cold. The least energetic, and physically the feeblest, although in some cases mentally the most acute, those of the warmest and dampest provinces. Doubtless original differences of race have contributed to these distinctive characteristics, but those of climate have also operated powerfully to the same end, in conjunction with those of food; and the nature of the people's food is itself in part determined by that of the climate. Thus wheat, which requires a cool climate, is the staple food of the middle classes in North-Western India; rice, which requires warmth and damp, that of all classes in Bengal and Burma; while in most parts of India the poorer classes live principally on the millets or even inferior grains that can be grown on poorer lands; and the very poor and generally weak races of the jungles of Chutia Nágpur depend largely on roots and wild fruits, the natural produce of the forests. Clothing and the structure of the people's dwellings also vary in like manner, being partly determined by the requirements of the climate, partly by the nature of the materials available. In Afghánistán woollen fabrics and sheep-skins are in general use, and the former are much worn also in the Punjab in the cold season by those who can afford them, while the poorer classes wear clothes padded with cotton wool. Cotton fabrics of varying texture are the ordinary clothing of all classes in India, and silks are very much worn in Assam and Burma; but the least civilised tribes of Chutia Nágpur, of the hills of Assam and Eastern Bengal, and the natives of the Andaman Islands, are able to exist with the smallest possible amount of clothing habitually worn by any of the human race. Again with regard to dwellings, in Balúchistán and also Afghánistán, where wood is scarce and rain comparatively rare, houses are built of sun-dried brick and mud, often with domed roofs of these materials, so as to dispense with wooden supports. In the drier parts of the Punjab and in Sind similar materials are employed, but wood being obtainable for rafters, the roofs are flat, covered with beaten clay; while in most parts of India houses are covered with sloping roofs of thatch or tiles to throw off the rain. In Cachar, again, where neither the summers are very hot nor the winters very cold, and abundant materials are afforded by the forests, houses are built entirely of wood or bamboos, with mats for walls, and thatched or mat roofs; and in Burma, where wood and bamboos are equally abundant, and the ground very damp, these materials alone are employed, the houses being raised on posts some feet above the ground surface.

Let us now take note of the more striking features of the climate of different parts of the empire. We have already seen that lying half within the Tropics, India is a very warm country, indeed one of the warmest on the globe. In Southern India and Ceylon, and also in Tenasserim, this is the case at all times of the year. The great difference between summer and winter in countries beyond the Tropics, as for instance in Europe and more particularly in Northern Asia, is due to two causes; first, that the sun is high in the sky in summer and low in winter; and second, that the summer days are much longer and the nights much shorter than those of the winter.[1] But in Southern India and Ceylon the noonday sun is never very low, and the difference in the lengths of night and day at any time of the year is small, and the less the farther south we go and the nearer we approach the equator. On the equator, day and night are each twelve hours long all the year round, and even at Point de Galle at the southern extremity of Ceylon, the longest and shortest days in the year differ by only forty-one minutes. At this place there is a difference of only 4° between the temperatures of the warmest and coolest months in the year, and the hottest day and coldest night in the year differ only by 19°. As we proceed northward all these differences increase, but as far north as Bombay those of temperature more rapidly in the east than in the west of the peninsula, and they are greatest in the heart of the country at a distance from the sea. Thus Mangalore on the west coast, Bangalore in the interior, and Madras on the east coast, are about equally far north of the equator, and the difference of their longest and shortest days is about one hour thirty-two minutes. But while the difference of the hottest and coldest months at Mangalore is only 7°, at Madras it is 12° and at Bangalore 13°. Even at Bombay, more than 400 miles north of Mangalore, this difference is only 9°; but beyond this it increases more rapidly in the west than in the east. Surat, which is only 160 miles north of Bombay, and Cuttack in Orissa are about in the same latitude, and there is a difference of 16° between the hottest and coldest months at Surat, and 19° at Cuttack; while at Nágpur between them, in the middle of the peninsula, it is as much as 26°. Still farther north again, at Hyderabad in Sind, there is a difference of 28° between the hottest

[1] For the explanation of these differences see *Phys. Geog.*, etc., chap. ii.

and coldest months, at Benares 30°; but at Silchar only 18°, therefore less than at Cuttack.

These differences at places equally far north, and therefore subject to the same variations in the lengths of the day and night, and in the sun's altitude; depend on the dampness or dryness of the climate. The damper the climate, the smaller is the difference of the summer and winter heat. That of the west coast of the peninsula is very damp, whereas most of the Madras districts on the east coast, and still more those in the interior, have a comparatively dry climate. But the driest part of the peninsula is the table-land around Bellary, the northern districts of Mysore, and that part of the Bombay Presidency that lies between the Western Ghats and Hyderabad State.

In northern India the contrast of dryness and dampness is even greater than in the peninsula. Sind, with the South-Western Punjab and Western Rájputána, is exceedingly dry; so much so that large tracts are desert and devoid of vegetation, and agriculture is very precarious, except where the land can be irrigated from the rivers. On the other hand, Cachar and Assam are the dampest provinces in India; they have no dry hot season like most other parts of India, and vegetation is green and luxuriant all through the year. Between these extremes the dampness of the climate increases gradually from west to east. Thus Eastern Rájputána, Central India, and the North-West Provinces are less dry than Sind and the Punjab, and their eastern districts less so than their western; Behar and Chutia Nágpur, which lie to the east of these, are still damper, and Bengal much more so, especially its eastern districts and those bordering on the sea. The dampness of the climate increases also everywhere on approaching the Himalaya, and lofty hills are always damper than the plains.

Owing to the dryness of most of North-Western India, its summer heat (in May and June) is greater than in any part of the peninsula. In some years the thermometer has been known to reach to over 120°, where well shaded from the sun; and in Sind and the Western Punjab, where there is very little rain in the summer, the afternoon temperature is little below 110° all through July, a heat that has very rarely been reached at Madras, even in the hottest years. On the other hand, the winters of North-Western India are cold, especially in the Punjab, where it sometimes freezes at night, and at one of the most northerly stations, Ráwalpindi, snow has been known to fall at this season.

In India, as in all other parts of the world, it is cooler on the hills than on the plains, and the colder the higher one ascends. On an average the temperature falls about 3° of the thermometer for each thousand feet of ascent. By ascending to a sufficient height, therefore, it is always possible to obtain a cool climate even at the hottest time of year. It is for this reason that stations called *sanitaria* (or health resorts) have been established on some of the higher Indian hills, such as Simla, Mussoorie, and Darjiling on the Himalaya, Shillong on the hills of Assam, Pachmarhi in the Central Provinces, Abu in Ràjputána, Matheran and Mahableshwar in Bombay, and Ootacamund on the Nilgiri Hills in Madras. Except Matheran these stations are between 3500 and 8000 feet above the sea. At greater elevations, which are to be obtained only on the Himalaya, the winter cold would be too great for comfort, and at any less elevation it is unhealthy at certain times of the year. At about 7000 feet the climate of the Indian hills bears some resemblance to that of Southern Europe.

We have seen that the west coasts of both peninsulas, and also Bengal and Assam have very damp climates, whereas North-Western India, and in a less degree, parts of the table-land of the peninsula are very dry. These differences depend chiefly on the character of the prevailing winds, since those which come from the sea are damp and bring rain, and those from the land are dry winds. And we have seen further that India has a great extent of land to the north, and a great extent of sea to the south. Generally, therefore, southerly winds are damp and northerly winds dry. There is indeed but little wind in India from due north, or in Northern India from north-east, for the Himalaya extends like a great wall along its northern frontier from north-west to south-east and then east, and shields it from any winds from those quarters. But winds of the same character come from the north-west, from the highlands of Afghánistán and Balúchistán, which are very dry countries; and these or west winds, which are from the same source, slightly changed in direction, blow all through the spring months as a rule in Northern India, and also down the west of the peninsula; so that this season is very dry in most parts of Northern India, and still more so in the Bombay Presidency; and it is owing to the prevalence of similar land-winds, not only at this time of year, but also when the rainy monsoon is blowing in other parts of India, that Sind and Western Rájputána are so arid and barren. On the other hand, the sea-wind, which is the rainy wind, blows chiefly from the south-west, and therefore full on the west coasts of India and Burma and the south coast of Bengal. These, therefore, are the dampest and most rainy provinces. And since rain is always more abundant on hills than on plains, and, as we have seen, ranges of hills run down the west coasts of both peninsulas and encircle Assam and Cachar, the rain of all these parts of India is exceedingly heavy, and the soil and air almost always damp. The wettest place known in the world, Cherra Poonjee, is on the hills between Sylhet and Assam, fully exposed to the south-west wind from the Bay of Bengal. But the sea-wind scarcely ever reaches Sind and Western Rájputána, and before it reaches the interior of the peninsula the south-west wind has to pass over the Western Ghats, which drain it of a great part of its moisture. Hence a further reason for the dryness of these parts of India.

In India, as in some other tropical countries, one season of the year is very rainy, and at another it scarcely ever rains, or if at all only in temporary showers. This change of seasons is marked by an entire and general change of the winds termed the monsoons.[1] In the winter, and in Northern and Western India all through the spring, the prevailing winds are more or less northerly or westerly, blowing from the land towards the sea, and are therefore dry and rainless; while from June to September, in Northern

[1] For an explanation of the monsoons, see *Phys. Geog. for Indian Schools*, chap. ii.

India, and up to December in Madras, sea-winds blow very strongly and bring much rain. At sea the winter wind is from the north-east, and is called the north-east monsoon, and the summer wind from the south-west, and is known as the south-west monsoon. In most parts of Northern India there is usually some rain in the early months of the year, when the land-wind ceases for a few days and is replaced by a southerly wind. This rain does not last long, but it is very important, since it enables the cultivators to raise two crops during the year; that of the summer rainy season termed the *kharíf*, and that of the winter the *rabi* crop. The wheat crop is exclusively a winter crop.

Plants and Animals.—While in the case of man his habits and welfare are greatly affected by the climate of the country in which he lives, in that of most other animals and of plants their very existence depends on it. Man by his skill and intelligence can so vary his habits of life as to live either in very hot or very cold climates. He can provide himself either with light or warm clothing, he can produce fire; and if the country to which he emigrates does not furnish him with the kind of food he is used to, he can almost always find some other kind equally capable of affording him nourishment. But most animals and plants are very limited in their powers of adaptation, and the struggle for existence among all is so severe that even a small change in the climate, in the kind of food available, or in the nature of the soil, often determines whether or not they can maintain their existence against their rivals and enemies. Hence, not only are many of the plants and animals of India such as occur only in India or in neighbouring countries with a similar climate, but the drier and damper parts of the country itself differ greatly in their vegetation and animal life, each having certain forms peculiar to it. Far more kinds of both flourish in a warm damp atmosphere than in its opposite, and thus the plants and animals of such damp provinces as Assam and Cachar, Arakan, Pegu, Tenasserim, and the Malabar coast of India, are more numerous and varied than those of any other part of the country; while those of Sind and the Punjab, except along the foot of the Himalaya, include but few kinds of either. To take a few examples. Palms of any kind grow

Fig. 2.—The Talipot and other Palms, Peradenia Garden, Ceylon.

only in tropical countries, or in the warmer parts of the

temperate zone, and most of them only in very warm and damp regions. The great Talipot palm (Fig. 2 *a*) grows only in the warm damp forests of Ceylon and Travancore. The cocoa-nut thrives only in the Tropics and near the sea, and grows best on the sea-shore. It is abundant all round the coasts of tropical India and of Ceylon, but nowhere far in the interior. The *tál* or Indian palmyra (Fig. 2 *b* and Fig. 24) will live in a hot climate where there is a long dry summer, but will not stand a cold winter, and accordingly is not found in the Punjab nor generally in North-Western India, though common elsewhere; while the date palm can withstand greater changes of temperature, requires but little water, and provided it can obtain this for its roots, grows best in a dry climate, even that of Sind. Two of the most valuable timber trees of India are the teak and the *sál*: now teak requires a warmer climate than sál and will not stand winter cold. Hence it is only in the hills of the Central Provinces that both these trees are to be met with; but the sál grows vigorously along the foot of the Himalaya, and forms considerable forests in Chutia Nágpur and the north-east of the peninsula, while teak is abundant on the Western Ghats, where the winter is not cold, and also in Burma as far north as lat. 25°, but not beyond. The *babúl* or gum-arabic tree and the sandal-wood both thrive in dry climates. The former occurs under these circumstances all over India, but the latter is restricted to Mysore and the adjacent districts of the Bombay presidency above the Ghats. Pines and cedars again are for the most part trees of cold climates, and most of the Indian kinds are found only in the Himalaya and the higher hills of Assam, and with but few exceptions not below 4000 or 5000 feet.

The plants and animals native to India, or commonly cultivated or domesticated, are so numerous that we can only mention a few of those most characteristic and familiar. Among the trees utilised for shade or ornament, and in some cases also for their fruits, the commonest are, besides the palms already mentioned, the banyan, with its numerous-rooting branches, the *pipal* or sacred fig-tree, the tamarind, the mango, the *ním*, the country almond, the jack, the *mahowa*, the fleshy flowers of which serve as food for man and beast, the casuarina, the *sisu*, the acacia-like *siris*, the graceful cork-tree (*Millingtonia*), and in dry countries the tamarisk; also the gorgeous flowering trees, the flamboyant or gold mohur-tree (*Poinciana*), the *jarul* (*Lagerstrœmia*) with its masses of purple blossom, the yellow and scarlet cotton-trees (*Bombax*), the crimson *dhák* or *palas*, the shoeflower-tree (*Hibiscus*), and the fragrant *champák* (*Michelia*), a favourite offering at the shrines of Hindu deities. Valuable timber trees are the teak, the sál, the toon, the babúl or gum-arabic tree, iron-wood, black-wood, sandal-wood, satin-wood, ebony, and in the Himalaya the deodar, box, and several pines. The indiarubber fig-tree is common in Assam and Upper Burma. Among the smaller but still conspicuous vegetation are bamboos, wild bananas, rattans, numerous flowering creepers, turmeric, orchids, aroids, and ferns including tree ferns, in the damper forests; in drier forests, thorny acacias, the bér-plum, and numerous acanthaceous shrubs; and on the still drier plains and hills, euphorbias and other euphorbiaceous plants, prickly pears (cactus), oleanders, asclepiads, and camel-thorn.

The commonest cultivated fruits are the mango, the banana or plantain, the orange, the pumplemoose or pummelo, the lime, the jack-fruit, the bér-plum, the guava, the papáya, the custard-apple, the water-melon, and many other gourds, the pine-apple, and in Northern India the lychee and the peach. The grape and musk-melon are only grown locally, and the apricot only on the hills of North-Western India. Of these the mango, banana, orange, jack and bér-plum, are indigenous to India, growing wild in the jungles.

The chief crop plants are, among food grains, wheat and barley in Northern India; rice, the wild form of which is indigenous, and which is everywhere grown in marshy ground, especially in Bengal, Madras and Burma; also maize, sorghum, and many other kinds of millet, which except in Bengal and Burma are the staple food of the agricultural classes. Among pulses, dál, gram, peas, and lentils; among oil-seeds, sesamum, mustard, rape, linseed, castor-oil seeds, cocoa-nuts, and ground-nuts. Among fibre plants, cotton universally, jute chiefly in Bengal, and cocoa-nuts for coir on the sea coast; for dye-stuffs, indigo, madder, safflower and arnatto; as condiments, chillies, ginger, turmeric, and cardamoms. And for food or stimulants, sugar-cane, arrow-root, tobacco, tea, coffee, Indian hemp, opium poppy, betel pepper, and the *supári* or areca-nut.

The animals of the Himalaya are for the most part different from those of the plains. Among them are the ounce or snow-leopard, the lynx, two kinds of bears, the yák, the ibex, the *markhor*, the *gooral* or Himalayan chamois, the *tehr* or wild goat, the *serow* or forest goat, the *burhel* or wild sheep, and the great wild sheep (*Ovis ammon*), the musk-deer, the Kashmir stag and the *Kyang* or Tibetan wild-ass, but some of these are restricted to the Western Himalaya or to great altitudes. In the Eastern Himalaya are the *shou* or so-called Sikkim stag, the cat-bear (*œlurus*), the *tákin* (*Budorcas*), and *mithan* or *gayal*, which do not range farther west.

On the plains and lower hills of India, the tiger, the leopard, several kinds of wild cats, civets, and palm-civets, the sloth bear, the hyena, wolves, foxes, jackals, and the so-called wild dog (*Cuon*), the elephant and wild hog, the *gour* or wild ox, the *arna* or buffalo, *nilghai*, four-horned antelope, sambur, swamp-deer, spotted deer, hog-deer, barking deer, and the diminutive mouse-deer are pretty general where either dense forest, thin bushy jungle, or rocky hills afford the kind of cover respectively suitable to them, but most of them do not extend to North-Western India. Monkeys of many different kinds are abundant. The Indian antelope or black buck is common on open plains, and the Indian gazelle in dry barren ground. The cheetah or hunting leopard is found in Central and Western and parts of Southern India; rhinoceroses of three kinds and a lemur in Bengal, Assam, and Burma, another lemur in Madras, and the gibbon, the *mithan*, and *binturong* or bear-cat in Assam; a wild ass in Sind, and the lion in Guzerat. Among the animals of Burma that do not occur in India are a gibbon, several monkeys, the Malay bear, the *banteng* and the *thameng* (*Panolia eldi*) with semicircular antlers, and a tapir.

The birds of India are very numerous, and not a few are

of kinds familiar to us in Europe, but one misses the little warbling songsters of our English woodlands, and is but poorly compensated by the more gorgeous plumage of the peacocks and jungle fowl of the Indian jungles, the hill pheasants, the parrakeets and green pigeons, the rollers, golden orioles, minivets, and the brilliant little sun-birds.

Among the most noticeable reptiles are the crocodiles, two kinds of which abound in the larger rivers and sometimes the tanks of India and Burma, attaining a length of 18 or 20 feet, and the *ghavial* or long-snouted crocodile, which occurs only in the Indus, Ganges and Brahmaputra, in the Mahánadi of Orissa and the Kuladán river of Arakan. The largest snake is the python, which occurs in all parts of India, though not common, and sometimes grows to 30 feet in length. More formidable than any of these are the venomous snakes, the largest of which, the *ophiophagus*, sometimes measures 12 feet in length, and is active and deadly. It is, however, less common than the smaller but equally deadly cobra, the Russell's viper, and the *karait*. The irascible little *echis* is only less fatal. The sea-snakes which abound on the shores of India and in some of the estuaries and lagoons are all very venomous.

According to an estimate drawn up by Mr. W. T. Blanford in 1881, the total number of known kinds of animals in India and its dependencies (not including the seas) amounts to upwards of 12,000. Of these 405 are mammals, that is, animals of such kinds as suckle their young, 1681 birds, 514 reptiles (snakes, lizards, tortoises, etc.), about 100 amphibians (frogs, toads, and newts), and 1357 fishes; the remainder being insects and other lower animals. In former days when forests were much more extensive, wild animals, especially of the larger kinds, were far more abundant than they now are, and probably more destructive of human life. But even now the loss of life from this cause is of appalling magnitude. In 1886 nearly 25,000 deaths of human beings were reported as caused by wild animals (including snakes) in India and Burma, and more than double that number of cattle. In the same year rewards, amounting to 189,000 rupees, were paid for the destruction of dangerous animals, viz. 1464 tigers,

4051 leopards, 1668 bears, 6725 wolves, upwards of 8000 other wild beasts, and 22,417 venomous snakes.

Population.—The census of India taken in 1881 showed that the population of India and British Burma amounted at that date to 253,982,595 souls (in round figures, 254 millions). Since then, the Empire has been increased by the annexation of Ava and the Burmese Shan states. Including their inhabitants, and allowing for the natural increase of the population at the rate of one to every 200 yearly, it is computed that in 1887 the total number was 268 millions.

The distribution of these in different parts of the country is very unequal. The general average in 1881 was 184 inhabitants per square mile, but in such provinces as Sind and the Punjab, where large tracts are too dry for successful cultivation and also in the Himalaya, there are thousands of square miles without a single inhabitant, while in such fertile districts as Behar on the plain of the Ganges, and Tanjore in the south, the population is very dense. It is, of course, most crowded in the cities. In Calcutta there were, in 1881, 87 inhabitants living on every acre, on an average, and 54,152 to the square mile; in Bombay, 52 to the acre and 35,142 to the square mile; and in Madras, which is a more scattered city than either, 29 to the acre and 15,031 to each square mile. In London there are nearly 60,000 to the square mile; but in London nearly all houses have at least an upper story, and the large majority two, three, or more stories, which is not the case in Indian cities, the houses of the poorer classes rarely having any upper story, and hence the Indian population is more crowded in its habitations than would appear from the comparison of these figures.

Apart from the cities, the densest population is that of Behar. In the district of Mozufferpore in this province there are 860 inhabitants to each square mile, and in that of Sarun 870. In Southern India, Tanjore is the most thickly populated district, and has 583 inhabitants per square mile. On the other hand, the hilly and jungly state of Bastar in the Central Provinces has but 15 inhabitants to the square mile, and the sandy and rocky waste of

Jeysulmere in Rájputána but an average of 6 or 7 souls to the square mile.

In stature, features, skin tint, and other racial characters, as well as in their intellectual and social development, the native inhabitants of the Indian Empire differ from each other in an extraordinary degree. They include tribes in the lowest as well as in the highest state of civilisation, and belonging to the most diverse races of mankind. The

FIG. 3.—MINCOPIE, ANDAMAN ISLANDERS.

lowest and most distinct are the Mincopie natives of the Andaman Islands (Fig. 3); very small black men of the negrito race, with round heads, and hair in little isolated tufts. Much advanced beyond these in the practice of domestic arts, since they build good houses and cultivate the land, but still in a savage state, are the people that inhabit the hill tracts of the Indo-Burmese frontier (Fig. 4). These are of Indo-Chinese race, of complexion varying from yellowish to brown, with high cheek-bones, narrow eyes, and lank hair. The hill people between Assam, Burma, and China, together with the Shans, Burmese (see Fig. 26) and nearly all the native inhabitants of the British possessions in the eastern peninsula, are of the same section of the human race, but many of them more advanced in civilisation.

The population of India proper, by which term we mean

FIG. 4.—NÁGÁ CHIEFTAIN.

the whole of the western peninsula and the plains west of the Brahmaputra, consists of (1) the dark aboriginal races, descended from the original occupants of the country at the time of the first Aryan invasion; (2) the fair, or at least lighter-tinted descendants of the Aryan and Scythian immigrants, who entered India from the north-west, probably in many successive waves, dating from a time long anterior to history; (3) mixtures of the two in all degrees of proportion ; (4) immigrants from the coasts, such as the Parsees, Jews, Arabs, and lastly the English and other Europeans ; and (5) Eurasians, the mixed descendants of Europeans and other races.

The aboriginal inhabitants include at least two distinct races, termed respectively Kolarian and Dravidian. They are distinguished, however, rather by their speech than their characteristic physiognomy. But even at the present day these races present many varieties of feature and stature, and they may possibly have descended from more than two original stocks. They are generally distinguished by their darker colour and broader features, and as a rule by their smaller stature. Some of the Oraons (Dravidians) of Chutia Nágpur are said to bear some resemblance to the negrito race, in the woolly crispness of their hair, their wide mouths, thick lips, projecting upper jaws, and flat noses, but these characteristics are by no means general. Aboriginal tribes, but little advanced towards civilisation, are to be met with in wild hilly districts in all parts of India ; but their chief home is in the broad belt of hill country that stretches across India from the Gulf of Cambay to the Bay of Bengal, and especially in Chutia Nágpur and the eastern districts and protected states of the Central Provinces. The lowest castes of Hindus in towns and villages throughout India are also of aboriginal descent.

The Aryan race is to be found in its greatest purity and its highest development in North-Western India, in the Punjab, Sind, and Rájputána, and in the mountains to the north of the former province, viz. in the Brahman inhabitants of Kashmir and the Jats and Rájputs. But they had penetrated in ancient times to all parts of India and Ceylon, forming the highest castes, and their members are distinguished by their fairer complexion and finely cut features (see Figs. 13 and 18). In the hotter and damper parts of the country they are less fair than in North-Western India, and less stalwart, and in some cases there may have been more or less intermixture of aboriginal blood, since the obstacle to such intermixture now opposed by the almost universal prevalence of caste was probably less deterrent in early times.

The communities of foreign origin who have reached India by sea are chiefly to be found on the west coast of the peninsula. They include the Parsees from Persia, the Portuguese of Goa, the black and white Jews of Cochin, and the Arab Moplas of Malabar. Except the first, the descendants of these are now very much intermixed with the races native to the country, while preserving their respective religions. The English and other Europeans of later immigration who have settled in the country and their half-caste descendants are more scattered, and are to be met with in most of the large cities. Those who have retired from Government service generally settle on the hills, where they have the advantage of a comparatively cool climate.

From this brief description it will readily be understood that the people of India proper consist of a number of races and tribes of most diverse origin, and that owing to the restrictions of caste, which rigorously prohibit intermarriage, they have not amalgamated to form a nation or even a number of nations, as, for instance, Celts, Saxons, Danes, and Normans have done to form the English and Scotch of to-day. Religious and sectarian differences have added to the original differences of race, so that at the present day as well as throughout her whole past history, while India has always been a collection of many countries, no one of these constitutes or has ever constituted a nation in the European sense of the term.

The population of Burma is more uniform; it includes several distinct tribes, but the great majority of these are of the same or nearly allied races, and the absence of caste distinction allows of their amalgamating to a greater extent than in India, at least in those parts of the country that are settled and civilised.

Many provinces of India and the countries beyond its north-west border take their names from the tribes that are or were once dominant in them. This is the case with such as have names ending in *stán* (*stán*, a place), *ána*, and *khand* or *kand;* and thus we have Hindústán (the place or country of the Hindus), now applied to the whole of India but formerly restricted to Northern India, the chief seat of the Hindu Aryans, to distinguish it from the Deccan (*Dakhin* or south); Rájastán or Rájputána (the country of the rulers, or the sons of rulers), the Rájputs having formerly ruled the whole of Northern India until they were dispossessed by Muhammadan invaders, and as a ruling race restricted to the tract which now bears their name or to native states scattered elsewhere. Also Gondwána, Telingána, Bundelkhand, and Rohilkand, which were respectively conquered or settled by Gonds, Telingas, Bundelas, and Rohillas.

Languages.—The latest census of the Indian people enumerates about 70 languages and dialects spoken in the British Indian Empire, exclusive of European and other foreign languages. With the exception perhaps of a few of those spoken by aboriginal tribes, all the native languages may be arranged under three distinct classes. First, we have such as are wholly or mainly derived from the Prakrit, which is the most ancient known form of the speech of the original Aryan immigrants, and is the rootstock of all the most prevalent languages of Northern India. It was the colloquial form of Sanscrit, and that dialect of Prakrit that was spoken in Behar is the language of the sacred Buddhist books of Ceylon and Burma, known as Páli. Second, the Dravidian languages, some form of which must have been spoken by the previous occupants of the country and was the root from which have sprung the Tamil and most of the other modern languages of Southern India, as well as of certain aboriginal tribes of Central India and Chutia Nágpur. Thirdly, the Indo-Chinese languages, which are those of the native inhabitants of Burma and of some of the hills that border Eastern Bengal.

These three classes of languages differ from each other in their essential structure and grammar more than any European languages, although the modern tongues derived from their respective roots and now spoken by the civilised inhabitants of India and Burma contain many words of Sanscrit origin; and all those that have a written character of their own have adopted some modification of those used by the ancient Hindus, the earliest forms of which, the Bactro Páli and Láth characters, are found in certain inscriptions on rocks, pillars, and Buddhist temples dating from the third century before the Christian era.

The language known as Urdú or Hindustani, which is spoken by most Indian Muhammadans and is the most general means of communication between Europeans and the natives of Northern and Western India, is a mixed language, derived chiefly from Hindi (the modern tongue of the Hindu inhabitants of the western half of the Ganges valley), but containing many Persian and Arabic words; and it originated at the time of the invasion of India by the Muhammadans. As a medium of intercourse between Europeans and educated natives it is now being superseded by English.

Religion and Caste.—In India proper, the dominant religions are Hinduism or Brahmanism and Muhammadanism, and in Burma, Buddhism. According to the census of 1881 there were in the whole empire nearly 188 millions of Hindus, over 50 millions of Muhammadans, and less than three and a half millions of Buddhists, but in consequence of the annexation of Ava, the civilised inhabitants of which are nearly all Buddhists, the last are now more numerous. There were also nearly two millions of Christians, about the same number of Sikhs, nearly one and a quarter millions of Jains, 85,000 Parsees or fire-worshippers, and 12,000 Jews. In addition to these adherents of recognised religions, there were nearly six and a half millions of aboriginals, whose religion is very primitive, and generally consists in the worship of anything that is strange or striking in nature, or in the propitiation of spirits and demons.

Four of these religions, viz. Hinduism, Buddhism, and those of the Jains and Sikhs, took their rise in Northern India, and all but Buddhism are now almost restricted to India. But Buddhism, which has spread from India to Ceylon, Tibet, and Burma, and all through Eastern Asia, has no longer any native adherents in the country of its birth. It was the dominant religion during the first three or four centuries of the Christian era, and the remains of massive reliquary mounds (*stupas*), monasteries and colossal images, sometimes sculptured in the solid rock (Fig. 5), which still exist in many parts of India, testify to its former power. Jainism, which is a modified form of Buddhism, probably branched off a distinct sect about the seventh or eighth century of our era. Its adherents are chiefly to be found in Western and Southern India. The Sikh religion was founded as late as the end of the fifteenth century, and is almost restricted to the Punjab; like Buddhism, it rejects all caste distinctions.

FIG. 5.—BUDDHIST CAVE-MONASTERY, AJANTA.

Among all Eastern nations religion dictates the practice and observances of daily life to a much greater extent than does Christianity those of Western nations; but Hinduism differs from all other modern religions in the degree in which it does this—in which it penetrates into and regulates the social relations and domestic habits of its adherents, and the rigour with which it enforces its decrees. Especially does it prohibit intermarriage and eating in common by members of different castes, and thus the Hindus instead of forming one community bound together by a common faith, are parted from each other and split up into a vast number of distinct units or castes, the limits of each of which are those of the social life of its members. The ancient writings of the Hindus speak of four castes only, the Brahmans or literate caste, the Kshetryas or warriors and rulers, the Vaisyas or trading caste, and the Sudras or labourers. But of these only the first is distinctly recognised among the modern inhabitants of India. It is true that the Rájputs and Khetris of to-day claim to be the descendants of the ancient Kshetryas, the Banias and Chettis those of the Vaisyas, and others those of the Sudras (probably the aborigines of ancient India); and it is very likely that in many cases these claims are well founded, but they are not universally recognised. At the present day the two highest castes are the Brahmans and Rájputs. In theory, a member of a lower caste cannot pass by adoption into one that is higher; but there can be no doubt that in past times, and to some extent even at the present day, additions have been and are made to both these castes by such transfers, though they are not recognised as equals and caste-fellows by the original communities of pure blood. On the other hand, members of the higher castes who have failed in certain caste observances have sometimes segregated as a sub-caste, while retaining their original appellation; and thus it has come about that these great castes include a very large number of sub-castes of very different degrees of social standing, fenced off from each other by disabilities similar to those that distinguished the original four castes.

The original castes were probably, in part, distinct tribes or races, and many of the modern castes must have had a similar origin. Thus the Mális, now known as gardeners, are possibly the descendants of the Malli who opposed Alexander in his march down the Indus valley; and the Ahírs (herdsmen), a very numerous caste in North-Western India, were probably originally a nomad tribe, though they are now largely cultivators. Again, almost every trade has its caste, and is practically in the hands of its members, though they are by no means necessarily restricted to it for their livelihood. These castes were probably, in their origin, associations of workmen having interests in common, like the trade guilds of Europe.

In addition to caste distinctions there are those of sect, and Hindu sects are very numerous. Some sects indeed reject all caste distinctions, but though this rejection may hold good among its own members, all such bodies are prone to separate as a distinct caste from the rest of the community.

Thus caste, as defined by competency to intermarry and to eat in company, is a form assumed by communities that have originated in many different ways, the result being that social isolation which is peculiarly characteristic of the people of India. In Burma, where there is no caste, the difference in this respect is very marked.

Products, Industries and Commerce.—We have already seen that India is above all things an agricultural country, perhaps the richest in the world; and at the present day its great and still increasing export trade, besides such valuable products as silk, tea, coffee, spices, drugs, and dye-stuffs, includes large quantities of wheat and rice, pulses, oil-seeds, cotton, and various vegetable fibres, hides, timber, and similar bulky produce of its fields and forests. Its mineral products, although not unimportant, are of less value than those of many countries of much smaller extent. Coal is extensively worked in Bengal, and to some extent in the Central Provinces, Hyderabad, and Assam. It occurs in what not many years ago were the wildest and most thinly-populated parts of the country, inhabited only by aboriginal tribes; and its working, while furnishing employment to these tribes, has brought about an extensive clearing of the forests, has attracted agriculturists to the newly-opened country, and has stimulated the construction of railways which carry the coal and the produce of the fields to distant markets. Petroleum has long been obtained in Burma, and is known to exist in Assam, the Punjab, and Balúchistán. Iron ores, some of great purity and richness, are widely distributed in India, and are smelted by very primitive processes by the natives. Copper, tin, and lead occur in places, but only in small quantities. Gold is found in the sands of many rivers, and the Soane (Són) of Central

India and Bengal, the Subanríka of Orissa, and the Subansiri of Assam take their names from the metal; but the produce is very small. Mines of gold are also worked in Mysore. Diamonds are still obtained in Bundelkhand, Chutia Nágpur, and the north of the Madras Presidency, but hardly repay the cost of working. Other gems, viz. rubies, sapphires, and many others of inferior value, are obtained chiefly in Ceylon and Burma, and sapphires in Kashmír. The Salt Range in the Punjab owes its name to the beds of rock-salt that occur in some parts of these hills, and the soil of certain tracts in Rájputána is so thickly impregnated with salt that the water of the Sámbhar lake and that of the Luni (salt) river is not brackish only, but absolutely salt. Notwithstanding this local abundance, the production of salt, as well as of all the other minerals previously enumerated, is insufficient for the wants of the country, and metals and useful minerals of all kinds are largely imported into India. The only important mineral export is saltpetre, and this, owing to the favourable conditions of the climate, is formed abundantly in the soil of old village sites, from which it is collected by washing.

As a manufacturing country, India is now in a state of transition; many of the old processes having nearly died out, and being only gradually replaced by the new. Before machinery driven by steam had been substituted for hand labour in spinning, weaving, and many other arts, the hand-woven cotton cloths, muslins, and silks of India not only supplied the clothing of the native population, but were largely exported to Europe. This has long ceased to be the case. Owing to their greater cheapness, machine-made European goods are now to be found in every Indian bazaar, and though the weaving of coarse cloths is still carried on in villages throughout the country, many of the most important native manufactures of former times are greatly depressed or nearly extinct. But India has the advantage of producing cotton and many other raw materials on the spot; and by importing machinery and establishing manufactories in places where coal can be obtained at a moderate price, the cost of transporting these raw materials to Europe and bringing back the manufactured goods is saved. This advantage and that of cheap labour have led of late years to some revival of Indian manufactures, and the production of cotton and woollen fabrics, both for local consumption and export, is already considerable, and is rapidly increasing.

In the production of rich and costly fabrics, such as carpets, silk brocades interwoven with gold and silver, embroidery, and fine figured muslins; also in jewelry, and ornamental work in metals, lacquer, and ivory and wood carving, India retains her ancient supremacy.

Some of the agricultural products of the country require to be manufactured on the spot, and these processes give a large amount of employment to the people. Such are the manufacture of indigo, tea, opium, shell-lac, and lac-dye. Of late years also there has been a considerable and increasing manufacture of cigars from tobacco grown in the country. Sugar and vegetable oils are extensively produced, but chiefly by simple native processes. These will, doubtless, in the course of time be superseded to a greater extent than at present by European methods, and thus in many directions the manufactures of the country may yet be much extended.

But except in the case of manufactured goods that are in local demand, and for which the country itself supplies the raw materials, it seems hardly likely that India will seriously compete with the workshops of Europe. Coal is dearer than in England, and though iron ores are abundant, iron smelting has not yet been successfully carried on on a large scale. Most other metals are not found in any great quantity in India, but have to be imported, and are therefore more expensive than in Europe. Moreover, Indian habits of life are comparatively simple, and change very slowly; and thus many things that are necessary to Europeans are not so to the natives of India. Articles of leather, glazed pottery and glass, and iron cooking pots, for instance, are but little or not at all used by the masses, and the few and simple household utensils they require are still made, as in former times, by the native artisans of villages and bazaars.

In 1887 the foreign sea trade of India consisted of exports to the total value of nearly 61 millions sterling of merchandise and $1\frac{1}{6}$ millions of treasure, and of imports to the value of more than 40 millions of merchandise and $7\frac{1}{2}$ millions of treasure. The value of the raw produce and manufactures exported from India therefore exceeded that of the imports by more than 20 millions sterling, while the imports of gold and silver exceeded the exports by $6\frac{1}{3}$ millions. In addition to these, there was imported on behalf of the Government stores to the value of more than a million sterling, of which nearly two-thirds consisted of materials for railways. About 95 per cent of this trade was carried on from the ports of Bombay, Calcutta, Madras, Rangoon, and Kurrachee, and 80 per cent from the first two named ports alone. Great Britain took 54 per cent of the whole trade, China 11 per cent, and France, which comes third in order, 7 per cent. Of the merchandise imported into India, cotton piece goods and yarn constituted one-half the value. Of the exports, the most important articles were grain (rice and wheat), raw cotton, opium (chiefly to China), seeds, hides, tea, jute, and indigo.

Great as this trade is, it is steadily increasing. In 1878, or nine years earlier, it was less than four-fifths as great, and the average increase has been at the rate of $2\frac{2}{3}$ millions a year.

In comparison with the foreign sea trade, that carried on with surrounding countries across the land frontiers is but small. In 1887 it amounted altogether to $6\frac{2}{3}$ millions sterling, of which about one-third was with Upper Burma, now a British possession. Next in importance was Nepal, which took more than one-fifth. The value of imports and exports across the frontiers were nearly equal.

Internal Communications.—Up to about the middle of the present century the internal communications of India were for the most part very primitive and defective. There were but few metalled roads suitable for rapid traffic, no railways and no canals, except one or two short lengths in Bengal and on the coasts. Except a few trunk lines the roads were mere tracks, impassable in bad weather, and travellers either walked or rode, exposed to all the dangers of Thugs and dacoits (gang robbers), or they were carried in palanquins, a slow and toilsome mode of conveyance. Merchandise and agricultural produce were conveyed on pack-bullocks or camels, or in rude carts drawn by bullocks, and the cost was such that, in times of dearth, it was impracticable to pour into the afflicted provinces the superabundant grain of those that had escaped the calamity. Owing to the circumstances of the climate and the form of the surface, very few of the large rivers of India are navigable. Rain, as we have seen, is almost restricted to one season of the year, and consequently the rivers are very full and rapid for a few months, and during the remainder of the year most of them are either shallow streamlets meandering through a waste of sand, or a string of pools and shallows. The Ganges, Brahmaputra, and Indus, and a few of their great tributaries, which receive the cold weather rainfall and the melting snows of the Himalaya, and for many hundred miles from their mouths flow through low plains, and the Irawadi in Burma, the conditions of which are similar, are the only streams that admit of extensive inland traffic. The Tapti, Nerbudda, and the great rivers of the peninsula, the Mahánadi, Godávari, and Kistna, are all of the former character; and since the upper part of their course is through high plains, with a rapid descent through the Ghats at a short distance from the sea, boats cannot ascend from the coast to their upper waters.

The construction of railways, which has progressed rapidly during the second half of this century, has necessitated that of good roads between them and the large towns and productive districts, and these improved means of communication have brought about great changes not only in the increase of commerce and in its distribution, but also in the civilisation of the people and the production of wealth; and they have transformed the aspect of many parts of the country. Many a district that only thirty or forty years ago was a wilderness of hill and forest, the inviolate haunt of the elephant, the wild ox, and the tiger, is now dotted over with coal-mines, giving employment to thousands of the aboriginals; or presents a rolling plain green with field crops, amid which, here and there, some gnarled forest tree, a remnant of the former jungle, is the only relic of its condition in bygone days. The produce of the mines and fields thus newly opened out are quickly carried to the markets of thickly-peopled provinces or to the ports of shipment, and thus the industry of the country is stimulated by the supply of coal, while in times of drought and scarcity the worst horrors of famine are averted, and in prosperous years the wealth of the country is increased by the sale to distant countries of the surplus produce of lands which have lain waste and unproductive for centuries. On the other hand, they have been the means of bringing within the reach of the people many conveniences and luxuries to which they were formerly strangers. Cheap clothing, machinery, utensils and implements of iron, copper and brass—or the metals for manufacturing these in India itself,—cutlery, paper, mineral oil for lighting, European drugs, tea, and a vast number of articles of less importance, which nevertheless subserve the convenience of the people and add greatly to their comfort, are now to be purchased in every bazaar, and are beginning to penetrate to the more remote and conservative population of the agricultural districts; and over and above these, precious metals to the value of nearly one hundred millions sterling have been poured into the country during the last ten years, in return for the produce exported to distant lands.

In March 1888 there were 14,383 miles of railway open for traffic; of which 8994 miles were the property of the Imperial Government, and 824 miles that of native states. In 1887 they carried upwards of 95 millions of passengers and 18½ millions tons of merchandise. This amounts to about one mile of railway to every 125 square miles of area on an average, and is but little when compared with the railway system of Great Britain, which in the same year had 19,812 miles of railway open, being an average of one mile to six miles of area. But the Indian system is extending at the rate of about 1000 miles a year.

The Government of India and its Provinces

The Supreme Government.—The supreme government of India consists of the viceroy and governor-general, assisted by an executive council of six members, all of whom are appointed by the Home Government. Their acts are subject to the general control of the Secretary of State for India in Council, the Secretary of State being a member of Her Majesty's Government. The seat of the government of India is Calcutta in the cold season, and Simla during the remainder of the year, and the headquarters of the several departments are distributed between the summer and winter capitals. A legislative council consisting of the governor-general and members of the executive council, the lieutenant-governor of the province in which its sittings are held, and certain other officials and non-officials selected by the governor-general, makes laws for the British territory as a whole, and exclusively for all provinces, excepting Bengal, Madras, and Bombay, which have legislative councils of their own.

Provincial Governments.—The Indian Empire having grown up gradually from small beginnings, exhibits in the administrations of its different provinces that variety that has resulted from the process of natural growth and the varying requirements of communities differing greatly from each other in the stage of their social advancement. In the provinces or presidencies of Madras and Bombay the head of the government is styled "Governor," and is appointed from home by the British Government of the day. He is assisted by an executive council and a legislative council, and although subject to the supreme government, his local government has very large independent powers. Bengal, the North-West Provinces, and the Punjab are under Lieutenant-Governors, and only Bengal has a legislative council. The Lieutenant-Governors are usually distinguished members of the Indian Civil Service.

In the Central Provinces, Assam, and Burma, which are more thinly-peopled and less advanced than the older provinces, the head of the local government is a Chief Commissioner, whose powers are less than those of Lieutenant-

Governors; and the official, termed Governor-General's Agent, who exercises a general supervision over the cluster of native states in Rájputána, exercises similar powers in Ajmere. The Resident of Hyderabad holds a similar position with regard to Berar, and the Resident of Mysore with regard to Coorg.

The province of Oudh is also a Chief Commissionership, but in this case the office is vested in the Lieutenant-Governor of the North-West Provinces.

The following is a list of the provincial governments of British territory:—

MADRAS	Governor and Council
BOMBAY	,, ,,
BENGAL	Lieutenant-Governor
NORTH-WEST PROVINCES	,, ,,
PUNJAB	,, ,,
OUDH	Chief Commissioner
ASSAM	,, ,,
CENTRAL PROVINCES	,, ,,
BURMA	,, ,,
BERAR	Commissioner
AJMERE	,,
COORG	,,

Native States.—About two-fifths of the empire consists of states under native rulers. These are of all sizes, varying from such large and important principalities as Kashmír and Hyderabad to the little hill states of the Punjab, one of which occupies no more than a single square mile. All are feudatory, either directly to the supreme government of India or to the provincial governments, and their native rulers are assisted and advised by officers of the British Government, termed Residents in the case of the larger states and Political Agents in that of some of the smaller, or they are under the superintendence of the Commissioners of the adjacent British territory. In the clusters of states forming Rájputána and Central India, and in Balúchistán, the Political Agents are subordinate to an official termed the Governor-General's Agent.

The following states are immediately under the administration of the Government of India. Those feudatory to the provincial governments will be noticed in connection with the several British provinces in which they are included.

Balúchistán.	Hyderabad.
Kashmír.	Baroda.
Rájputána Agency.	Mysore.
Central India Agency.	

Foreign Possessions.—The only foreign nations that retain possessions in India are the French and Portuguese. The former have five settlements, the chief of which is Pondicherry. The governor of this territory is also governor-general of the French possessions in India. The Portuguese retain three settlements, the chief of which is Goa. They are administered by the Portuguese governor-general, who resides at Goa. All of these will be briefly noticed at the end of this work.

THE PROVINCES OF INDIA

Balúchistán

Area, 160,500 square miles. Population, 400,000

Name and Government.—Balúchistán (the country of the Balúchis), in so far as it forms part of the British Empire, is subject to the Khan of Kalát, to whom a number of other chiefs are tributary; the western portion had been absorbed by Persia before the demarcation of the frontier. Three small districts only are British, and are administered by the agent of the governor-general as commissioner.

General Features.—Except a narrow strip of coast plain and the Kach Gandava desert between the Indus and the foot of the Khirthar range, the whole of Balúchistán is a part of the great Irán table-land, which it shares with Persia on the west and Afghánistán on the north. On the east this table-land terminates to the west of the Indus valley in the Khirthar and Sulemán ranges, on the south in the Makrán range running parallel with the coast. The highest part of its surface is in the east, where the valley plains are between 5000 and 6000 feet above the sea, and it has a gentle slope westwards and northwards from the Makrán range, in which directions flows the scanty drainage of the hills till it loses itself in swamps in the central desert. On the banks of the Helmand in the north-west corner of Balúchistán the elevation is below 2000 feet. The whole of the country is remarkably arid, being beyond the reach of the Indian summer monsoon, and its chief rain or snow-fall is in the early months of the year. The hills therefore present a bare surface of stratified rocks, in which every outcrop stands out distinctly as in a geological diagram, and the valleys between them are grassless plains of loam fringed with gravelly slopes, and fertile only where they are irrigated by water brought long distances in underground channels termed *karezes*, to prevent evaporation. The northern part is a desert plain dotted with salt swamps.

Position and Area.—Balúchistán occupies a roughly rectangular tract of about 160,500 square miles, between the meridians of 60° 40′ and 69° 45′ E. long., and between 24° 50′ and 30° 20′ N. lat. Its extreme length from east to west is 545 miles, and its extreme breadth from north to south 374 miles.

Mountains and Rivers.—The eastern half of the country is intersected with parallel ranges of hills running generally from north-east to south-west; in the Khirthar and Sulemán ranges this direction changes to nearly north and south, and in the Mari and Bhúgti hills connecting them, to east and west The southern half is crossed in like manner by ranges running nearly east and west, parallel with the coast. The average height of the main southern or Makrán range is between 4000 and 5000 feet. That of the Khirthar rarely exceeds 3500 feet in lower Sind, but rises gradually northwards to between 4000 and 5000 feet, and where it enters Balúchistán, between the Kach Gandava desert and Kalát, it has several peaks between 7000 and 8000 feet. To the north-east of Quetta, somewhat beyond the range, are two of 11,000 and 11,750 feet. The Sulemán range averages 7000 feet and culminates in the Takht-i-Sulemán (Solomon's throne) at 11,300 feet.

Owing to the dryness of the country there are no large rivers in Balúchistán. The most important is the Helmand, which skirts its north-western border, draining the mountains of Western Afghánistán and discharging itself into the Sistán lake. The Lora river from Quetta and the Shirináb from Kalát unite and flow to the south-west, losing themselves in a salt swamp. A few small streams from the Khirthar range and the Mari and Bhúgti hills reach the plain to the west of the Indus, the margin of which they serve to irrigate. The best known of these is the Bolan, which gives its name to the well-known pass which is the main route of communication between Sind and Candahar.

Administrative Divisions.—The British districts are Pishín, Quetta, and Sibi; the two former to the north-west and north of the Bolan Pass, the last including all the hill country north of the Kach Gandava plain. Native or Kaláti Balúchistán is divided into seven districts. The Makrán on the south includes the greater part of the coast plain and the adjacent hill ranges that border the table-land. Lus is the extreme eastern corner of this tract, adjoining Kurrachee. Jhaláwán (the lower country) occupies the south-eastern part of the table-land; Saráwán (the upper country) the higher plateau to the north of it, lying to the west of upper Sind; and Kalát, adjacent to both, the district immediately around the capital. Kach Gandava consists of the plain between Jacobabad in Sind and the foot of the Khirthar range on the west, and the Mari and Bhúgti hills on the north; and Kohistán (the mountain country) is the western part of the plateau adjoining Persia.

Towns.—Kalát, the capital, is situated on the valley plain of the Shirináb river, to the west of the Khirthar range, at 6780 feet above the sea. Quetta or Shál (the fort) on the similar plain of the Lora river, 84 miles farther north and 5500 feet above the sea, is the headquarters of the governor-general's agent, and now an important military station, strongly garrisoned for the protection of the Southern Afghánistán frontier. It commands the Bolan route and communicates by two lines of railway with Jacobabad. Fifty miles to the north-west is the frontier post Chamán at the foot of the Khojak range, where the railway now terminates. There is no good harbour on the coast, but Gwádar close to the Persian frontier is a port of call for the Persian Gulf steamers.

Population.—The population of Balúchistán is estimated at 400,000. They consist mainly of two races, speaking different languages, the Brahuis and the Balúchis, of whom the former are the rulers. The hills north of the Kach Gandava plain are peopled by the Maris and the Bhúgtis. The people are all Muhammadans.

Productions.—Among minerals, antimony, copper, lead, sulphur, and petroleum are known to occur, and the last is being worked by the British Government with a view to obtaining fuel for the railway. The scarcity of water much restricts agriculture, but where this is obtainable the usual Indian crops are raised; also apricots, peaches, grapes, almonds, pistachio-nuts, apples, pears, plums, and several other fruits. Camels are extensively bred by the Balúchis, and serve as the ordinary means of transport. There are no manufactures of any importance.

Railways.—The frontier post of Chamán communicates with the Indus valley system by two lines of railway which branch off between Pishín and Quetta and meet again at Sibi, not far from the entrance of the Bolan Pass. One of these, on the broad gauge, runs through the Chapar rift to Harnai, and descends to the plain through the Nari Pass. The other, on the narrow gauge, passes through Quetta and descends by the Bolan Pass. From Sibi to Jacobabad in Sind a single line on the broad gauge crosses the Kach Gandava desert.

KASHMÍR

Area, 68,000 square miles. Population, 1,500,000

Name and Government.—Kashmír (Cashmeer) is so called from a legendary being who is supposed to have drained the valley. Strictly the name applies only to the far-famed Vale of Kashmír, but it is now used to designate the whole of the state ruled by the present Rajah. This ruler is of Rájput family, descended from Golab Singh, an officer of Runjit Singh's, to whom it was transferred on the annexation of the Punjab. A British officer, the Resident, represents the Government of India at his capital.

General Features.—Kashmír consists almost wholly of lofty table-lands, mountains, and valleys, including some of the highest ranges of the Himalaya, and the beautiful valley of world-wide fame which was the favourite summer retreat of the Mogul emperors of Delhi. The "Vale of Kashmír," once filled by an ancient lake, is now a fertile plain, 84 miles long, from 20 to 25 broad, and at a mean elevation of 6000 feet above the sea; it is traversed by the Jhelum river, here navigable for a distance of 60 miles, and surrounded by lofty snow-capped mountains. On the south and south-west it is cut off from the plains of the Punjab by the Pír Panjál range, crossed by passes between 11,000 and 12,000 feet; and on the north and east it is enclosed by the Zánskár range, which divides it from the valley of the Upper Indus.

The mountain region to the north and east of the valley is physically a part of Tibet. The north-eastern part consists of broad flat valleys and gravelly plains from 13,000 to over 17,000 feet above the sea, uninhabited and almost bare of vegetation. They are crowned with mountain ranges, which as seen from these heights appear but small, but really average 20,000 feet, with peaks varying up to 28,000 feet, and which send down some of the largest glaciers in the world. The Indus river traverses the whole region from south-east to north-west, during which it descends from a height of 13,700 to 4000 feet, flowing in a deep valley between two lofty ranges. Everywhere beyond the crest of the Zánskár range the climate is very dry. At Leh in the Indus valley the whole rain and snowfall of the year is less than 3 inches, and it rains or snows on an average on only one day in fifteen. There are but few trees, and except in Astor and parts of Baltistán, no forest; and the agriculture of the valleys (chiefly barley, buckwheat, and millet, with some wheat) depends entirely on irrigation. Owing to the dryness of the air, the climate is one of fierce extremes, the excessive heat of the summer days alternating with night temperatures below the freezing-point, while the winters are very severe. It contrasts strongly with the mild, genial climate of the Kashmír valley, which resembles that of Southern Europe.

Position and Area.—Kashmír is the most northerly part of British India. It reaches to N. lat. 36° 30′, which is almost exactly that of Cape Matapan, the most southerly point of Europe. Its southern limit is in lat. 32° 21′, and it lies between 73° 27′ and 80° 32′ E. long. It extends 300 miles from north to south, and 384 miles from east to west, and covers an area of 68,000 square miles, of which the valley occupies not more than 1500. On the north it is bounded by the Chinese province of Káshghár, on the east by that of Tibet, on the north-west by the little independent hill states of Hunza, Yasín, and Chilás, on the west by the Hazára, Ráwalpindi, and Jhelum districts of

FIG. 6.—THE GREAT BÁLTORO GLACIER.

the Punjab, on the south by the Punjab plains, and on the south-east by Chamba, Láhul, and Spiti.

Mountains and Rivers.—The principal mountain chains of Kashmír and of the North-West Himalaya generally have a north-west and south-east direction. These are (1) the Pír Panjál range nearest the plains of India; (2) the Zánskár or Bára Lácha range to the north-east of the Kashmír valley, beyond which it continues to the Sutlej, forming the boundary between Zánskár and Rupshu on the north-east and the native state of Chamba and the Kángra district of the Punjab on the south-west; (3) the Ladákh range to the north of the Indus; and (4) the Mustágh or Kárákoram range also north of the Indus, dividing Kashmír from Káshghár or Chinese Turkestan. This last is the highest. Its principal pass, the Kárákoram, by which traders travel to Káshghár and Yárkand, is 18,317 feet above the sea or 2600 feet above the summit of Mont Blanc. Eighty miles to the west of this pass is Mount Godwin Austen (28,265 feet), which, next to Mount Everest in Nepal, is the highest known mountain in the world; and near it are other peaks over 25,000 feet. From this range descend the two enormous glaciers, the Báltoro (Fig. 6) and the Biafo glaciers, the former 36 miles long. To the south of the Indus, on the common border of Kashmír and Chilás, another great mountain, Nanga Parbat, rises to 26,629 feet.

The chief rivers of Kashmír are the Indus, with its great tributary the Shayok; the Jhelum, and the Chenab. All these rivers in the upper part of their course run parallel with the mountain chains from south-east to north-west; but subsequently they turn to south-west, breaking through the mountains and escaping to the plains of the Punjab. This peculiarity, as well as other facts of the mountain structure, show us that the rivers are older than the mountains, and existed before the mountain chains were upheaved; and further, that the mountains must have been raised so slowly that the rivers were enabled to cut down and deepen their valleys, keeping pace with the upheaval. The Shayok receives the melting snows and glaciers of the south-west face of the Kárákoram range and the north-east face of the Ladákh range, and breaking through the latter joins the Indus above Skárdo. The Indus, which rises in Tibet to the north of the sacred lakes Manasorawar and Rákas Tál, enters the Rupshu district of Kashmír in E. long. 79° 10′, flowing at an elevation of 13,700 feet above the sea, and then runs north-west in a deep valley through Ladákh and Baltistán, a distance of 320 miles, leaving the latter at an elevation of 4000 feet. Its subsequent course, partly to south and partly to west, is through independent states up to the point where it enters the Hazára district of the Punjab. It receives the drainage of the north-eastern face of the Zánskár range, that of the Ladákh range, and that of the Kárákoram range (chiefly through the Shayok), and also that of a great tract of mountains in Yagistán beyond the north-western frontier of Kashmír, through the Gilgit river. The Jhelum rises at the south-eastern extremity of the Kashmír valley, flows to north-west through the valley, and then turning to south-west, breaks through the Pír Panjál at Baramula. The Chenab, here called the Chandra Bhága, enters the Jummoo district of Kashmír from Chamba, and turning from north-west to west breaks through the Pír Panjál and makes its exit on the Punjab plain above the town of Jummoo.

In the Kashmír valley are a few marshy lakes, the remnants of the great lake that at one time filled it. The largest of these is the Walar lake near Srinagar, about 10 miles by 6. In Rupshu and the high plains and valleys in the north-east of Ladákh are several salt lakes, the remains of larger lakes of fresh water that existed at some former time when the country was less dry and the snowfall greater than at present. They are gradually drying up.

Administrative Divisions.—For administrative purposes the country is divided into the districts of Kashmír proper, *i.e.* the valley; Jummoo, the mountains to the south and south-east; and Punch, those to the south-west. All these are south-west of the Zánskár range. Also the governorships of Ladákh and Gilgit, the latter to the north-west of the Kashmír valley, the former comprising all the high mountain country around the Indus valley north-east of the Zánskár range.

Towns.—The chief towns are Jummoo (Jamu), the capital and seat of the native government, situated at the foot of the Himalaya, on the Tavi river, near the point where the Chenab issues from the mountains; Srinagar (Sirinagar), the former capital of Kashmír and now the summer residence of the Maharajah, on the banks of the Jhelum, about midway in the Kashmír valley, 5235 feet above the sea; and Leh, the capital of Ladákh, in the Indus valley, 11,500 feet above the sea. It is the residence of the governor of the province and of a British officer termed the joint-commissioner, appointed to watch over the trade between India and Turkestan; for Leh is an important centre of trade, inasmuch as nearly the whole trade between India and Chinese Turkestan passes through it. Skárdo is the chief town of Baltistán, on the Indus, 150 miles below Leh, and Gilgit on the Gilgit or Yasín river, a frontier fort beyond the Indus.

Population.—The population of the Kashmír territory is about 1½ millions. They consist of (1) Mongolians (allied to Tibetans and Chinese) in the north-east and east, and (2) various Aryan races (allied to the people of Northern India) in the north-west and everywhere south of the Zánskár range. The Mongolians are Buddhists in Ladákh, and Muhammadans (Baltis) in Baltistán. The Aryans of the Gilgit and Astor valleys west of Baltistán are Dards, a peculiar race who also people the various states of Yagistán beyond the frontier, and are all Muhammadan. The lower class Kashmíris (of the Kashmír valley) are Muhammadans, but probably of the same race as the higher classes who are Hindu Brahmans. The people of the south-eastern mountains, between the Zánskár range and the outer hills, are Hindus of various tribes, locally known as Paháris (mountain people). Those of the outer hills between the Kashmír valley and the Punjab plains are also Hindus, known as Dogras in the south and Muhammadan Chibhalis in the west. The rulers of the country are of the Dogra race.

Several different languages are spoken in Kashmír. In Ladákh and Baltistán two dialects of Tibetan, Kashmíri in the valley, Dogri and Chibhali in the mountains of Punch and part of Jummoo, and several dialects of Pahári in the valleys of the Chenab and its tributaries. In Gilgit there are three or four dialects of Dardi.

Productions.—The ordinary field crops of Kashmír are the same as those of the Punjab—wheat, barley, rice, maize, and millets being the chief grains. In Ladákh and Baltistán barley is the chief food grain, with buckwheat and certain hill millets. Most fruits of the temperate zone thrive in the Kashmír valley; among them the grape, from which is made the only wine produced in India. The forests of the Chenab valley yield valuable deodar timber. Among minerals, sapphires are found in Kishtwár, borax in the Puga valley, and salt in Rupshu. The most important manufacture is that of shawls and cloth (*pashmína*), made from the *pashm* or fine wool produced chiefly by a breed of goats in the high valleys in winter. Ornamental work of silver and copper, and also of papier-maché is manufactured at Srinagar.

The Punjab

Area, 142,449 square miles. Population, 22,712,120

Name and Government.—The Punjáb (five waters) is so named from the five great tributaries of the Indus which descend from the Himalaya, and after traversing the province unite in the Panjnad (five rivers) which joins the Indus at its south-western corner, above Mithankot.

The head of the administration is the Lieutenant-governor, and the seat of government is at Lahore during the cool season and at Simla in the summer.

General Features.—About five-sevenths of the province consists of the alluvial plain formed by the five rivers and the Indus. It is the most northern portion of the great Indo-Gangetic plain already noticed at p. 14. At Siálkot, near the foot of the Himalaya, it is 850 feet above the sea, and at Mooltan, 250 miles to the south-west, about 400 feet; so that, although apparently flat to the eye, it really slopes to the south-west on an average about $1\frac{4}{5}$ foot per mile. The strip of plain between the Indus and the Sulemán mountains is termed the Derajat, and the five wedge-shaped segments included between the Indus and the five rivers, termed *Doábs* (two waters), are named in order from west to east.

1. The Sind Ságar doáb between the Indus and the Jhelum.
2. The Chaj doáb between the Jhelum and the Chenab.
3. The Rachna doáb between the Chenab and the Ravi.
4. The Bári doáb between the Ravi and the Beas and lower Sutlej.
5. The Jullundur doáb (the smallest) between the Beas and the Sutlej.

The plain east of the Sutlej extending to the Jumna has been included in the Punjab province since 1857. It was formerly known as the Cis-Sutlej districts of the North-West Provinces. It is crossed by another river, the Saraswati or Sursati, which once formed a sixth tributary of the Indus, but now loses itself in the Rájputána desert. It was on the banks of this river that the Aryan Hindus first settled. The tract between it and its tributary the

Ghaggar was the Brahmavarta, the holy land of the Hindus.

Within about 100 miles of the Himalaya, where in most seasons there is sufficient rain for the crops, and elsewhere wherever it can be irrigated, this plain is very fertile. But farther south, where the rainfall is light and uncertain, all the higher ground is uncultivable. Some tracts are useful as grazing grounds and are covered with a dry scrub of leafless bushes and a few stunted trees, and the remainder is covered with sandhills, or with a barren saline soil termed *reh*; and such water as is obtainable, only from wells 150 to 200 feet deep, is salt and unfit for drinking. Partly by means of canals led off from the great rivers, and partly from wells, there were, however, in 1887, not less than 10,370 square miles of irrigated land in the Punjab, a greater extent than exists in any other province of India.

To the east of the Jhelum the Punjab plain reaches up to the foot of the Himalaya; but to the west of that river only up to the foot of the Salt range. This range of hills is so named from its containing thick beds of rock-salt. It runs east and west with a strong southerly curve from Jelálpur on the Jhelum to Kálábágh on the Indus; and to the west of the Indus runs first to the south and then once more westward to join the Sulemán mountains, which form the boundary of the province and of British India. The country to the north of the Salt range is a table-land, called the Pátwar to the east of the Indus, and in some places is as much as 2000 feet above the sea. It consists chiefly of soft sandstone rocks, and much of its surface has been cut into deep ravines by the streams that drain it; the Indus river crosses it in a deep gorge from Attock to Kálábágh.

About 60 miles north of the Salt range another lower range of hills, the Márgalla and Chíta Pahár range, crosses the Pátwar in a curve parallel with the Salt range, and to the north of these hills a plain surrounded by mountains extends on both sides of the Indus. Like the Kashmír valley it is the bed of an ancient lake. The Pesháwar plain to the west of the Indus is crossed by the Kabul river and leads up to the Khaiber pass, which is the chief route between India and Afghánistán, and through Afghánistán to Central Asia. Alexander and most of the subsequent invaders of India entered India by the Pesháwar plain. A few miles farther north, the mountains on both sides close in on the Indus, which here re-enters British territory. The Pátwar table-land and other high plains north of the Salt range occupy about one-seventh of the whole province.

The remainder of the province, also about one-seventh of the whole, comprises two tracts of the Himalaya, one to the west, the other to the south-east of Kashmír. The first consists of the narrow valley of the Kunhar torrent which flows into the Jhelum, and that of the Siran, a small tributary of the Indus, together with the outermost hill range of the Himalaya between the Jhelum and the Pátwar table-land. The second includes the valley and head-waters of the Upper Ravi, those of the Upper Chenab, the Beas, and a long stretch of the valley of the Sutlej and its tributary the Spiti river; also the upper valley of the Tons, which flows into the Jumna. It thus includes all the mountains south-west of the Zánskár range and south-east of the Kashmír governorship of Jummoo, and on the east it is bounded partly by Tibet and partly by Garhwál, a district of the North-West Provinces. Only the valleys and the lower hills of these mountain tracts are inhabited. Above 7000 or 8000 feet there are but few inhabitants on the mountain slopes, but in the valleys there are villages up to 10,000 and 11,000 feet above the sea-level.

Position and Area.—The whole province has an area in round figures of 142,500 square miles, and measures 530 miles from north-east to south-west, and 560 miles from north-west to south-east. It lies between the parallels of 27° 37′ and 35° 10′ N. latitude, and between 69° 34′ and 79° E. longitude; therefore wholly outside the tropical zone. 106,632 square miles, or about three-fourths of the whole, are directly administered by the British government of the province, and the remainder is divided between thirty-six native states, feudatory to the local government. Thus the country directly administered by the lieutenant-governor of the Punjab is only 15,000 square miles less than the total area of the British Isles, and, together with the included native states, 21,000 square miles greater. Nearly three-quarters of the former, or 76,000 square miles, are on the lower plain, 15,000 square miles on the Pátwar table-land and the other high plains north of the Salt range, and an equal amount in the Himalaya or the lower hills that form the border of the mountain country. Of the territory under native rule 25,000 square miles are on the plain, and nearly 11,000 square miles in the mountains.

Mountains and Rivers.—On the west, north, and north-east, the Punjab plain is girt round with mountains. The Sulemán range on the west runs north by east and south by west; the Himalayan ranges on the north-east have a general direction from south-west to north-east; and the Salt range, the Chíta Pahár, and the spurs that run down parallel with these from the outer Himalaya, linking the two former together, are curved between east and west and north-east and south-west.

As we have seen in the description of Kashmír, the great rivers, in the upper part of their course, flow in valleys that separate the great mountain ranges and run parallel with them; but afterwards break through them and make their exit on the Punjab plain, where eventually they all unite in the Indus.

The Indus enters the Punjab at Amb, receives the Kabul river from the Pesháwar plain on the west, and then enters a gorge at Attock. From Attock to Kálábágh, where it leaves the Salt range, its fall is very rapid, and it can be navigated only by skilled boatmen. Above Kálábágh it receives the Sohan river, which drains the greater part of the Pátwar, and 30 miles below, the Kurram river from the Western mountains. Again, 70 miles farther south, it receives the Gomal from the Sulemán mountains and Afghánistán. These are the only important tributaries down to its junction with the Panjnad, which brings to it the combined waters of the five Punjab rivers.

The upper course of the Jhelum in the Kashmír valley has already been noticed (p. 56). After breaking across the Pír Panjál range it forms the boundary of the Punjab and Kashmír for about 100 miles, flowing southward between the Pír Panjál and the outer Himalayan range, the Murree hills. It leaves the mountains a little above the town of Jhelum, turns the eastern extremity of the Salt range, and then enters the Punjab plain. It is navigable below Jhelum. Below Jhang it unites with the Chenab.

The Chenab rises in the snowy mountains at the head of the Láhul valley. It here bears the name of the Chandrabhága, and is formed by the junction of two main streams, the Chandra and the Bhága. It flows north-west through Chamba into Kashmír, where it breaks through the Pír Panjál and enters the Punjab plain near Jummoo.

The Ravi is a smaller stream. It rises in snowy mountains at the head of the Chamba valley, turns round the end of the Dhauladhár range, and after forming the boundary of Kashmír for nearly 30 miles, flows out on the plain. It joins the Chenab 50 miles below the junction of the Jhelum.

The Beas rises in the snowy range at the head of the Kulu valley, flows for 100 miles westward, cutting through the outer Himalayan hills, and then crosses the plain to its junction with the Sutlej, 30 miles south of Amritsar.

The Sutlej, next to the Indus the greatest of the Punjab rivers, takes its rise in the sacred lakes Manasorawar and Rákas Tál in Tibet, enters British territory at Shipke in a deep gorge in which it is joined by the Spiti river, flows westwards across the whole of the Himalaya, and after a diversion to the south in the outer Himalaya enters the Punjab plain at Rupar. It then resumes a westerly course across the plain, joins the Beas, and turning to the south-west receives no other affluent for a distance of 270 miles up to its junction with the Chenab to form the Panjnad. Forty miles below, this last unites with the Indus.

The Sursati and Ghaggar collect the drainage of only the outer Himalaya between the Sutlej and Jumna, and uniting about 80 miles from the hills, strike westward past Sirsa till they disappear in the desert. Except in the rainy season they present dry channels beyond a few miles from the hills.

Lastly, the Tons drains the valleys east of Simla and south of the Bashahr snowy range, which bounds the Sutlej valley. It unites with the Jumna at its exit from the Himalaya.

Administrative Divisions.—About three-fourths of the province are directly administered by the lieutenant-governor and the British officials under him, the remainder being feudatory native states. It is divided into ten commissionerships, usually termed divisions, and these again into thirty-two districts as follow, each under a deputy-commissioner :—

Divisions.	Districts.	Area. Sq. Miles.	Population.
Peshâwar	Peshâwar	2504	592,674
	Hazára	3039	407,075
	Kohat	2838	181,540
Derajat	Bannu	3868	332,577
	Dera Ishmail Khan	9296	441,649
	Dera Gházi Khan	4517	363,346
Ráwalpindi	Ráwalpindi	4861	820,512
	Jhelum	3910	589,373
	Gujrát	1973	689,115
	Shahpur	4691	421,508
Mooltan	Jhang	5702	395,296
	Montgomery	5574	426,529
	Muzaffargarh	3139	338,605
	Mooltan	5880	551,964
Amritsar	Siálkot	1958	1,012,148
	Gurdáspur	1822	823,695
	Amritsar	1574	893,266
Lahore	Goojránwála	2587	616,892
	Lahore	3648	924,106
	Ferozepore	2752	650,519
Jullundur	Kángra	9069	730,845
	Hoshiárpur	2180	901,381
	Jullundur	1322	789,555
Umballa	Simla	18	42,945
	Ludhiána	1375	618,835
	Umballa	2570	1,067,263
Hissar	Sirsa	3004	253,275
	Hissar	3540	504,183
	Rohtak	1811	553,609
Delhi	Karnál	2396	622,621
	Delhi	1276	643,515
	Gurgaon	1938	641,848

The districts to the west of the Indus, in order from north to south, are Pesháwar, Kohat, and Bannu (part), north of the Salt range; Dera Ishmail Khan (part only) and Dera Gházi Khan on the Derajat plain. Hazára consists of the mountain tract and some small included plains between the Indus and Kashmír. The Ráwalpindi district is the northern half of the Pátwar, together with the hills on its northern border. The southern half and the greater part of the Eastern Salt range form the Jhelum district; the remainder is included in Bannu.

The districts of the Punjab plain west of the Sutlej are Gujrát, Siálkot, Gurdaspur, and Hoshiárpur along the foot of the Himalaya. Bannu (part) and Shahpur at the foot the Salt range. Dera Ishmail Khan (part), Jhang, Lahore, Goojránwála, Amritsar, and Jullundur in the central tract, and Muzaffargarh, Mooltan, and Montgomery, all very arid districts, in the south.

The greater part of the Punjab Himalaya south of Kashmír forms the district of Kángra, including Láhul, Kulu, and Spiti. The little district of Simla lies south of the Sutlej, surrounded by native states.

Finally, the plain between the Sutlej and the Jumna, besides a number of native states, includes the districts of Ferozepore, Ludhiána, and Umballa on the north, Sirsa and Hissar on the south-west, and Karnál, Rohtak, Delhi, and Gurgaon on the east.

Native States.—Thirty-six native states are feudatory to the Government of the Punjab, and occupy a total area of 25,000 square miles on the plains and nearly 11,000 square miles in the mountains. The largest in size, but only second in population, is Baháwalpur, under a Muhammadan ruler. It extends along the Sutlej and Indus south of Mooltan. Ten states, the largest and most populous of which is Patiála, are on the eastern plain between the Sutlej and the Jumna. The most important of these, Patiála, Jind, and Nábha, are under Sikh rulers, distinguished, together with the Jat ruler of Kapurthala, for their active loyalty to the British Government in the darkest hour of the mutinies of 1857.

The remainder are hill states; two of them, viz. Chamba,

in the valleys of the Ravi and Chenab, and Bashahr in the Sutlej valley, are each over 3000 square miles in area. The others are less important.

Fig. 7.—The Kutab Minár at Delhi.

Towns.—The two chief cities are Lahore and Delhi. Lahore, the capital and seat of government, with a population of 149,000, of whom more than half are Muhammadans. It stands about a mile from the present course of the Ravi, on the margin of the cultivated tract of the Bári doáb. It was for a time the capital of the Mogul emperors, and later, that of Runjit Singh, the Sikh ruler, and contains his palace and tomb. Delhi, with 173,000 inhabitants, of whom 95,000 are Hindus, on the right bank of the Jumna, on the low ridge which marks the northern extremity of the Arvali range of hills. It is one of the most ancient cities of India. Ruins of former capitals surround modern Delhi to a distance of 20 miles. The great mosque, the Jama Masjid, and the fort and palace, which are its finest buildings, were erected by the Emperor Shah Jehan. The great tower, the Kutab Minár (Fig. 7), the loftiest column in the world, 240 feet in height in its present truncated state and 50 feet in diameter at its base, is 11 miles from the modern city. It is believed to be 700 years old.

The other more important towns, with the exception of Mooltan, lie along the northern border of the province. They are Pesháwar (80,000), the great mart and garrison of the north-west frontier, opposite the Khaiber Pass; Ráwalpindi (53,000), 8 miles from the foot of the Himalaya on the Pátwar plain, an arsenal and large military station; Siálkot (46,000), another important military station, 72 miles north of Lahore; Amritsar (pool of nectar) (152,000), the holy city of the Sikhs, so named from the tank, in the centre of which stands the golden temple of the Sikh faith; it is the centre of the Kashmír shawl trade, and is itself a seat of the manufacture; it is the wealthiest and, next to Delhi, the most populous city of the Punjab; Ludhiána (67,500), a fort and cantonment near the south bank of the Sutlej; and Umballa (44,000), a great commercial city and military station, whence a railway is now being constructed to the foot of the hills opposite Simla.

Mooltan (68,500), in the south-west of the province, 4 miles from the Chenab, the capital of the Malli at the time of Alexander's invasion. It produces a well-known *faïence* pottery, and is the centre of the trade between the Punjab and the Sind port of Kurrachee.

The two most important hill-stations of the Punjab are Simla (7200 feet above the sea), the summer seat of the

Viceroy's Government, and also of the Lieutenant-Governor of the Punjab; and Murree (7000 feet), five hours' journey from Káwalpindi, overlooking the Pátwar; it is the chief sanitarium of the North-Western Punjab.

Population.—In 1881 the population of the Punjab

FIG. 8.—PATHÁNS.

was nearly $22\frac{3}{4}$ millions; of whom nearly 19 millions were directly under the British Government of the province. This gives an average of 159 to the square mile, but large tracts of the mountains and the southern plain are uninhabited.

Of the inhabitants of the plains the greater part are Jats and Rájputs (see Fig. 13), chiefly Muhammadans in the west and Hindus in the eastern districts. In the former,

Patháns (Fig. 8) from the western hills are also numerous. The Sikhs who, before the annexation of the Punjab, were the ruling sect, form 6 per cent of the population, living chiefly in the centre and east of the province. The Punjabi language is a dialect of Hindi. In the high valleys of Spiti and Láhul the people are of Tibetan race and language, and Buddhist by religion. Among the lower hills of Kángra and Sirmúr they are Hindus.

Productions.—The salt mines of Pind Dádun Khán in the Eastern Salt range are perhaps the largest in the world, and have been worked since the time of Akbar. Other important salt mines are at Káläbágh on the Indus and in Kohat to the west of that river, where a bed of rock-salt 1000 feet thick is worked. Wheat is the chief agricultural export, but all the ordinary field crops of Northern India are raised in the Punjab. The hill-forests furnish a large supply of deodar timber, and boxwood and the pencil-cedar occur in the interior of the hills. Pine-wood is abundant above 5000 feet. Fine teas are produced in the Kángra valley.

The more important manufactures are shawls at Amritsar and Ludhiána, woollen, silk, and cotton fabrics and embroidery; glazed pottery is made at Mooltan, Pesháwar, and Delhi; wood-work inlaid with ivory and brass at Hoshiárpur, cutlery and damascened work at Wazírabad and Gujrát.

Railways.—The North-Western Railway runs from Delhi through Meerut to Sahâranpur, both in the North-West Provinces; then recrossing the Jumna it passes Umballa, Ludhiána, Jullundur, and Amritsar to Lahore. From Lahore, one main line runs north to Gujrát, Jhelum, and Ráwalpindi, and crossing the Indus at Attock, continues past Nowshera to Peshâwar opposite the entrance of the Khaiber Pass. Another main line from Lahore runs to the south-west down the Bári doáb to Mooltan, and is continued as the Indus Valley Railway through Baháwalpur to the Sind frontier at Reti. A line that will shortly be completed, the Delhi and Kalka Railway, runs direct from Delhi to Umballa, and on to Kalka at the foot of the Himalaya, whence an excellent road of 58 miles leads to Simla.

The branch lines of this system are: one from Amritsar running northward to Patliánkot at the foot of the Himalaya, giving access to the hill-stations Dalhousie and Dharmsála, and to the numerous tea-gardens of the Kángra valley; another that takes off from the main line at Wazírabad, on the right bank of the Chenab, and leads to Siálkot and Jummoo, the capital of Kashmir; a third branches off between Gujrát and Jhelum, and runs along the foot of the Salt range to the salt mines of Pind Dádun Khán, and on to the Indus, where it meets the Sind Ságar loop-line, which runs down the left bank of the Indus to opposite Dera Gházi Khan, with a short branch to Muzaffargarh, opposite to Mooltan; a fourth leaves the main line near Ráwalpindi, and runs west along the foot of the Chíta Pahár range to Kushalgarh, on the bank of the Indus, opposite to Kohat with its salt mines. All these lines are on the broad gauge.

Another railway system, on the narrow gauge, connects Delhi with the districts to the west. It runs south-west to Rewari, whence the main line continues southwards to Ráǰputána and Bombay, and a branch leads off to the north-west, passing through Sirsa and terminating at Ferozepore on the right bank of the Sutlej, only 50 miles distant from Lahore.

North-West Provinces and Oudh

Area, 111,236 square miles. Population, 44,849,646

Name and Government.—The North-West Provinces were so named before the annexation of the Punjab, when they formed the north-western portion of the old Presidency of Bengal. The kingdom of Oudh, named after the ancient city Ayodia, was placed under the same government in 1877. It was previously a separate government under a Chief Commissioner, residing at Lucknow, and this style is retained, the Lieutenant-Governor of the North-West Provinces being Chief Commissioner of Oudh.

General Features.—Excepting a stretch of 180 miles of the Himalaya between the Punjab and Nepal, and a small tract of higher rocky ground to the south of the Jumna, the whole of this province lies on the alluvial plain watered by the Ganges and its affluent rivers; and next to Bengal proper it is the richest and most populous division of British India. The soil of the plain is formed of the fine silt which in the course of ages has been brought down by the flooded rivers, and deposited as their flow was checked by the spread of their waters over the surrounding flats; and with a rainfall varying from 25 to upwards of 50 inches in different parts of the plain, and, in general, abundant means of irrigation from wells or canals fed by the rivers, there are but few portions that are not capable of yielding two crops annually to the tillage of its industrious peasants. As seen from any point of vantage, it presents a vast plain of fields dotted over with villages and fruit-bearing and other trees. But it is by no means a uniform level. Besides being gently sloped from the foot of the Himalaya to the course of the main river, and from west to east, each of the larger streams has excavated a broad channel in the older sandy deposits, which were formed when they flowed at a higher level; so that the greater part of the surface is now permanently above the reach of the heaviest floods, and these tracts, termed *bhángar* land, depend for watering either on the rainfall or on irrigation from wells or canals. The lower lands watered directly from the rivers are termed *khádar* land. In the west, and especially between the Jumna and Ganges, in the Gangetic doáb, where the rainfall is less than 30 inches, the soil in certain places is so charged with salts left by evaporation as to be uncultivable. These tracts are termed *reh* or *usar*. Similar soils occur also under like circumstances in the Punjab.

The Himalayan portion of the province consists of the mountains between the Tons and the Sárda rivers, and includes the whole of the valleys drained by the Ganges and Jumna. The Tons river separates the North-West Provinces from the Punjab, the Sárda from Nepal; and the mountain range that forms the northern water-parting of all these river basins, separating them from that of the Sutlej, is the frontier of British territory, and the Tibetan district of Nari-Khorsum or Hundesh.

The tract to the south of the Jumna is chiefly a part of the valley of the Betwa river. It is but little raised above the plains, and is dotted over with a few little hills and hummocks of hard crystalline rocks, but is not otherwise hilly. Only in the south-east of the province, in the Mirzapur district, it includes some low ranges of hills, with a part of the valley of the Són (Soane) river.

Position and Area.—The total area of the province is 111,236 square miles, including 5125 square miles of native states, chiefly in the Himalaya. But the whole of these Himalayan native states and British districts together occupy but 16,000 square miles, and the districts on the higher rocky ground south of the Jumna and Ganges about 17,500. The remaining 78,000 square miles, or between two-thirds and three-fourths of the whole province, is the arable land of the Gangetic plain. This plain has an average width of 160 miles, and so much as is comprehended in the North-West Provinces and Oudh, an average length of 480 miles. The extreme length of the province from north-west to south-east is about 500 miles, the extreme width 300 miles. It lies between 77° 4′ and 84° 45′ E. long., and between 23° 51′ and 31° 5′ N. lat.; therefore wholly outside the tropic.

Mountains and Rivers.—To the south-east of the Sutlej the Himalaya is a less complex system of mountains than to the north-west of that river. Instead of the three more or less continuous chains of snowy peaks already briefly noticed in Kashmír, a single chain, which we may call the Garhwál range, runs to the south of the Sutlej, forming the boundary of the North-West Provinces and Tibet, and sending off great spurs to the south-west towards the plains of India. On these spurs rise a succession of great peaks—Badrináth, the Trisúl, Nanda Devi, etc., between 22,000 and 26,000 feet in height, separated by the valleys of the Ganges, the Sárda, and their tributaries, which rise from the glaciers of the Garhwál range.

Along the base of the Himalaya and parallel with it, runs a low range of hills, the Siwáliks or Sub-Himalaya, enclosing a series of flat valleys termed dúns (doons). The highest parts of these are about 2000 feet above the sea, and to the north of them the Himalaya rises abruptly to 6000 or 7000 feet. It is on the outer spurs of the Himalaya, overlooking the plains, that are situated the favourite hill-stations and military sanitaria, Chakráta, Mussooree, Landour, and Naini Tál.

The rivers of the North-West Provinces and Oudh are all tributaries of the Ganges. On the north, the chief of them are the Jumna, the Ganges, the Rámganga, the Sárda, the Gogra, the Rapti, and the Gandak, which bring down the drainage of the Himalaya ; and the Gumti, which drains

FIG. 9.—THE GANGES AT DERALI.

the plain of Oudh between the Ganges and the Gogra. On the south, the Chambal, the Betwa, the Ken, the Tons, and the Són (Soane) from the central Indian plateau. Excepting the Betwa, only a small part of the lower course of these latter rivers lies within the province.

The Jumna rises at the Jamnotri glacier, and after issuing from the mountains receives the Tons from the Punjab, then runs southward across the plain past Delhi, forming the boundary of the North-West Provinces and the Punjab. At Agra it turns to the south-east and flows close to the southern margin of the plain up to its junction with the Ganges at Allahabad, receiving successively the Chambal, the Sind, the Betwa, and the Ken rivers.

The source of the Ganges is at the Gangotri glacier of the Garhwál range, a famous place of pilgrimage. It here bears the name of the Bhagirathi. It traverses the outer Himalaya (Fig. 9), and just before issuing on the plains unites with the Alaknanda, an equally large river, also from the Garhwál range. It breaks through the Siwáliks at Hardwár, another famous place of pilgrimage, and then runs across the plain, first to south then to south-east, receives the Rámganga below Fatehgarh, and unites with the Jumna at Allahabad. After passing Benares it receives the Tons on the south and the Gumti from Oudh, and leaves the North-West Provinces at its junction with the Gogra.

The Rámganga rises in the hills of Almora, and in its course across the plain of Rohilkand receives several small affluents from the outer Himalaya to the eastward, and falls into the Ganges below Fatehgarh.

The Sárda takes its rise in the Garhwál range to the east of Nanda Devi, and in its southward course through the mountains forms the boundary of the North-West Provinces and Nepal. After leaving the Himalaya it runs to the south-east across the plain of Oudh, where it takes the name of the Chowka, and falls into the Gogra.

The source of the Gogra is in Tibet, north of the Garhwál range, near that of the Sutlej, and to the south of the great lake of Rákas Tál. It cuts across the whole of the Himalayan range and continues southward across the plain of Oudh, till it receives the Chowka north-east of Lucknow. Then turning to south-east it traverses the eastern districts of the North-West Provinces and falls into the Ganges at Chupra. For the last 50 miles of its course it forms the boundary of the North-West Provinces and Behar.

The Gumti is not a Himalayan river. It drains the plain between the Rámganga and Ganges on the one hand, and the Chowka and Gogra on the other, and falls into the Ganges some miles below Benares.

The Rapti has a more tortuous course. Its head waters are the streams that drain the southern flank of the great

Dhaulagiri, and unite in a river that first flows due west between that mountain and the outer Himalaya; then, breaking through the latter, it bends sharply to the south-east, and after a course of 180 miles across the plain of Oudh and Gorakhpur unites with the Gogra.

The Gandak (Gunduk), a very large river from Nepal, only skirts the north-east corner of the North-West Provinces, and will be more fitly noticed among the rivers of Bengal.

The rivers that come down from the Himalayan range have some water at all times of the year, and the larger streams are navigable, but the southern tributaries of the Ganges and Jumna are dry or nearly so in the hot season. They are also smaller, the rainfall of Central India being in some parts as low as 20 inches and in none much exceeding 50 inches in the year. Only the Betwa has any considerable portion of its course in the territory of the North-West Provinces. It rises on the crest of the Vindhya escarpment within a few miles of the main stream of the Nerbudda, and runs nearly north through the native state of Bhopál, and the North-West Provinces districts of Lalitpur and Jhánsi, after which it turns to the east and falls into the Jumna at Hamírpur.

Administrative Divisions.—The North-West Provinces and Oudh are divided into eleven divisions or commissionerships and forty-nine districts, the areas and populations of which are as follow:—

Divisions.	Districts.	Area. Sq. m.	Population.
Meerut	Dehra	1193	144,070
	Saháranpur	2221	979,544
	Muzuffernagar	1656	758,444
	Meerut	2379	1,313,137
	Bulandshahr	1915	924,822
	Aligarh	1955	1,021,187
Agra	Muttra	1453	671,690
	Agra	1850	974,656
	Farrukhabad	1718	907,608
	Mainpuri	1697	801,216
	Etáwah	1694	722,371
	Etah	1739	756,523

Divisions.	Districts.	Area. Sq. m.	Population.
Rohilkand	Bijnor	1868	721,450
	Moradabad	2284	1,155,173
	Budaun	2002	906,451
	Bareilly	1614	1,030,936
	Sháhjahánpur	1746	856,946
	Pilibhit	1371	451,601
Allahabad	Cawnpore	2370	1,181,396
	Fatehpur	1639	683,745
	Banda	3061	698,608
	Hamírpur	2289	507,337
	Allahabad	2833	1,474,106
	Jaunpur	1554	1,209,663
Benares	Azamgarh	2147	1,604,654
	Mirzapur	5224	1,136,796
	Benares	998	892,684
	Ghházipur	1473	1,014,099
	Gorakhpur	4598	2,617,120
	Basti	2753	1,630,612
	Ballia	1145	924,763
Jhánsi	Jhánsi	1567	333,227
	Jalaun	1469	418,142
	Lalitpur	1947	249,088
Kumaon	Almora	6000	493,641
	Garhwál	5500	345,629
	Tarái	938	206,993
Lucknow	Lucknow	989	696,824
	Unao	1747	899,067
	Bara Banki	1768	1,026,788
Sitapur	Sitapur	2251	958,251
	Hardoi	2312	987,630
	Kheri	2992	831,922
Fyzabad	Fyzabad	1689	1,081,419
	Bahraich	2741	878,048
	Gonda	2881	1,270,926
Rae Bareli	Rae Bareli	1738	951,905
	Sultanpur	1707	957,912
	Partabgarh	1436	847,047

The first six divisions are included in the North-West Provinces, the last five in Oudh. The Kumaon division consists of the Himalayan districts, together with the swampy tract (the Tarái) at the foot of the mountains. The Meerut division is the northern part of the doáb between the Jumna and Ganges; the Agra division the central doáb, together with a tract of country around

Muttra and Agra on the right bank of the Jumna. In the Allahabad division, Cawnpore, Fatehpur, and part of Allahabad district occupy the lower doáb; Banda and Hamírpur the tract opposite on the south bank of the Jumna; and Jaunpur and part of Allahabad lie north of the Ganges below the confluence of the two rivers. Rohilkand, so called from the Rohilas (hillmen), an Afghan tribe who settled in the country in the middle of the last century, consists of the northern plain between the Ganges and the Sárda, up to the borders of Oudh. Oudh, an independent kingdom up to 1856, occupies all the central portion of the plain north of the Ganges. The Benares division includes the districts east of Oudh up to the Gandak river on the north and the junction of the Gogra and Ganges on the south, together with the district of Mirzapur, which lies south of the Ganges and extends across the Kaimúr hills and the Són river southward to the hills of Chutia Nágpur. The Jhánsi division lies wholly south of the Ganges, and consists of a strip of the central Indian plateau wedged in between the native states of Málwa and those of Bundelkhand.

Native States.—There are two native states feudatory to the North-West Provinces government, viz. Tehri Garhwál (4180 square miles), which occupies about one-fourth of the Himalayan territory of the province, and Rámpur (945 square miles), on the plain of Rohilkand, under a chief of Rohila descent.

Towns.—In the North-West Provinces and Oudh there are six cities with upwards of 100,000 inhabitants, a larger number than in any other Indian province. These are—Benares (200,000), on the Ganges below Allahabad, dating from the earliest Aryan occupation of the Ganges valley, and in all historic times, as well as now, the metropolis of Hinduism. It contains 1454 temples, among them the golden temple dedicated to Shiva; but few, if any, are of great antiquity, and indeed the present site of the city is not that which it occupied in ancient times. The stone ghats on the north bank of the river are very fine (Fig. 10). Lucknow (261,000), on the right bank of the Gumti, the capital of Oudh, and the former residence of the

Nawábs; famous for the heroic defence of the Residency under Sir Henry Lawrence, the relief of its garrison by Outram and Havelock, and its withdrawal by Sir Colin Campbell in 1857. Agra (160,000), on the right bank of the Jumna below Delhi, the capital of Akbar and Shah Jehan, also the seat of the provincial government from 1835 to 1857. The Táj Mehál (Fig. 11), the mausoleum

FIG. 10.—BENARES.

of Shah Jehan and his wife Mumtáz-i-Mehál, a domed building in white marble with the interior richly decorated in mosaic, is one of the most beautiful buildings in the world. Cawnpore (151,000), on the right bank of the Ganges due south of Lucknow, with a garden and memorial church commemorative of the massacre of its garrison together with "a great company" of women and children, in 1857, by the orders of Nana Dhoondu Panth, better known as Nana Sahib. Allahabad (148,000), so named by Akbar, also known by its Hindu name, Prayág, at the junction of the Ganges and Jumna; the seat of the provincial government since 1857; also a place of Hindu pilgrimage. In the fort is a column bearing an inscribed edict of Asoka of the third century B.C. Bareilly (113,000), in Rohilkand, on the Rámganga, 96 miles above its confluence with the Ganges.

Other places of importance are—Meerut (99,500), the chief military cantonment of the province, on the Gangetic

FIG. 11.—THE TÁJ MEHÁL, AGRA.

doáb, 40 miles north-east of Delhi: Muttra (Mathura) (47,500), on the right bank of the Jumna between Delhi and Agra, an ancient Hindu city, the scene of Krishna's youthful adventures, and now the centre of the Vaishnava sect of Hindus; remarkable for the beauty of its Hindu architecture: Roorkee (11,000), the headquarters of the engineering staff of the Ganges canal, and the chief engineering school of India: Moradabad (67,000), in Rohilkand, well known for its niello brass ware: Aligarh (60,000), in the doab, north-east of Muttra, the seat of an institute founded by an enlightened Muhammadan gentleman, Syud Ahmed, for the instruction of his co-religionists and others: Mirzapur (56,000), on the right bank of the Ganges between Allahabad and Benares, a great centre of trade in agricultural and forest produce.

The chief hill-stations are Naini Tál (6409 feet), in Kumaon, situated at the head of a small mountain lake, the summer seat of the provincial government. Mussooree (6881 feet), on the crest of the outermost ridge of the Himalaya, overlooking the valley of Dehra Dún; and Chakráta (7051 feet), Landour (7500 feet), and Ránikhet (6069 feet) established as military sanitaria.

Population.—In 1881 the population of these provinces amounted to nearly 45 millions, or 403 souls to the square mile on an average. Of these, 86 per cent were Hindus and 13 per cent Muhammadans. Brahmans are most numerous in the Benares, Allahabad, and Agra divisions; Rájputs chiefly in Benares and Agra; and Baniyas (the trading caste) in the Upper doáb, Agra, Meerut, and Allahabad. Of the lower castes, Chamárs (leather-workers) number upwards of 5 millions, Ahírs (herdsmen) 3½ millions, Kúrmís (often classed with Mális as gardeners) 2 millions, and Kahárs (palki-bearers) 1¼ millions. There are 300 less numerous castes. There are nearly 700,000 Játs (probably the same as the Jats of the Punjab), chiefly in the western districts bordering on the Punjab. The cultivators include members of all castes.

The language of the province is Hindi.

Productions.—The agricultural produce of the Gangetic plain includes all the ordinary field crops of India. Wheat is everywhere the chief crop of the cold season, rice being grown only in the rains and on low-lying (*khádar*) lands. Grain and oil seeds are largely exported. The opium poppy is grown chiefly in the eastern districts for the manufacture of opium at the Government factory at Gházipur. Tea is largely grown in Kumaon and the Dehra Dún. There is little forest except in the Himalaya, where valuable deodar forests exist in Tehri Garhwál, and fine sál forests on the *Bhábar* or dry gravelly slopes at the foot of the mountains.

Cotton fabrics plain and printed are produced in many of the large towns, and rich brocades of silk interwoven with gold and silver (*Kinkháb*) at Lucknow and Benares; also jewelry. The brass ware of Benares and Moradabad are well known in Europe. Cawnpore is the chief seat of leather manufacture and cotton weaving.

Railways.—The principal line of railway and the only line with fast mail trains is the East Indian, from Calcutta to Delhi, which, in the North-West Provinces, follows the right bank of the Ganges up to Cawnpore, and then strikes across the Gangetic doáb to Delhi. It passes through Mirzapur, Allahabad, Cawnpore, and Aligarh, and sends off short branch lines to Benares, Agra, and Muttra, and a main branch from Allahabad to Jubbulpore as part of the mail route from Calcutta to Bombay. From Gháziabad, opposite Delhi, the North-Western Railway continues the main line to Meerut, Sahéranpur, and the Punjab. Another railway system is that of the Oudh and Rohilkand Railway, which connects with the North-Western and East Indian Railways at Sahéranpur, Aligarh, Cawnpore, and Benares. From Sahéranpur it runs through Roorkee and Moradabad and meets the line from Aligarh at Chandausi; thence on to Bareilly, Sháhjahánpore, and Lucknow, where it is joined by the branch from Cawnpore; and from Lucknow through Fyzabad, Sultanpur, and Jaunpur to Benares. Branches from this line lead northwards, viz. from Roorkee to Hardwár, from Bareilly to Pilibhit, and also to the foot of the Himalaya below Naini Tál. A loop railway also runs from Cawnpore to the Hatras station of the East Indian Railway, following the right bank of the Ganges, another line from Cawnpore south-west to Jhánsi and Bhopál, and two railways from Agra run southwards into Rájputána and Central India.

Bengal

Area, 187,222 square miles. Population, 69,536,861

Name and Government.—Bengal (Bangálah) the name first used in the fourteenth century for the delta of the Ganges and the plain to the north, is derived from Banga, the original name of the tract east of the delta. The old name of Bengálah was Gaur, from the ancient capital some distance to the north of the Ganges, now ruins buried in jungle.

The province of Bengal in its present extended sense includes the eastern half of the Gangetic valley, the combined deltas of the Ganges and Brahmaputra, and the alluvial plain of Orissa, together with a great extent of highlands to the west of the delta and south of the Ganges, and a strip of hill country to the east of it, also bordering the Bay of Bengal. In a more limited sense, Bengal is the name of only the deltaic portion and the plain to the north stretching up to the foot of the Himalaya. The plain west of this strip up to the confines of the North-West Provinces, that south of the Ganges traversed by the Soane (Són) river, and the hilly country between this and the delta constitute Behar; and Orissa is the name given to the coast plain on the north-west corner of the bay, formed by the deltas of the Mahánadi and some smaller rivers from the western highlands. The great stretch of hill country to the west of the delta and south of Behar is termed Chutia Nágpur. Bengal is under a lieutenant-governor, who ordinarily resides at Calcutta. Before 1854 the governor-general of India was governor of Bengal.

General Features.—Owing partly to its proximity to the sea, partly to the network of rivers that intersect the delta, and the flat swampy nature of its surface, the climate of Bengal is damper and the extremes of heat and cold less than those of the Upper Provinces, and it is the richest and most productive as well as the most populous province of India. To the north of the delta and on the plains of Behar are large stretches of high (*bhángar*) land as in the North-West Provinces, but the low-lying *khádars* are wider, and of the deltaic tract only small isolated portions are permanently and but little above flood level. With but few exceptions the whole of this plain is richly cultivated, chiefly with rice. The southern margin of the delta to a distance of 30 or 40 miles inland, termed the Sunderbuns (Forest of Sundri trees), is an uninhabited swampy forest, intersected with creeks and subject to inundation at high tides. Chutia Nágpur and a part of southern Behar are elevated and hilly, consisting of hard crystalline rocks which rise in places to rocky hills of considerable height and enclose basins of valuable coalfields. Up to the middle of this century nearly the whole of this country was a very wild tract of hill and forest, tenanted by aboriginal tribes, and Chutia Nágpur is still so in a great measure; but a good deal of the northern portion has been cleared and cultivated, and the native population have for the most part settled in fixed villages, or are employed as workmen in the coal-mines.

The strip of country east of the delta and of the Bay of Bengal is also high, but consists of soft sandy and shaley rocks, which, a few miles inland, begin to rise in lines of hills running north and south and gradually increasing in height. The interior of this country, known as Tipperah and the Chittagong hill tracts, is peopled by races of Indo-Chinese origin, often predatory, and only gradually being brought into peaceful habits of life. It is still covered with forest, and only the lower strip along the coast is settled and civilised.

Of the Himalaya north of Bengal only a very small part, consisting of the ridges and valleys drained by the Teesta, and wedged in between Nepal and Bhotan, is included in the province, and the greater part of this is occupied by the feudatory state of Sikkim.

Area and Position.—The total area of Bengal is 187,222 square miles, of which 36,634 square miles (nearly one-fifth of the whole) is occupied by native states. It is somewhat less than Spain, more than half as large again as the British Isles. 99,000 square miles, or more than one-half, are on the plains of the Ganges, Brahmaputra, and the Orissa rivers. The remainder consists of the uplands of south Behar and Chutia Nágpur, the Chittagong hills and a small tract of the outer Himalaya around Darjiling. It extends 560 miles from north by east to south by west, and 700 miles from west by north to east by south. The most northern point in the province is in lat. 27° 15′, the most southern in lat. 19° 25′. About one-third of the whole lies south of the Tropic of Cancer and therefore within the torrid zone.

Mountains and Rivers.—The greater part of the

Himalaya north of Bengal is included in the kingdom of Nepal, the remainder in Sikkim and Bhotan, excepting a small area of the outer hills around Darjiling. Its leading features are similar to those of Garhwál and Kumaon, already described. There is a line of lofty peaks about 80 or 90 miles from the plains, and these are separated from each other by the valleys of rivers that take their rise in a lower but continuous line of elevation farther north, and this latter divides the Himalayan drainage flowing into the Ganges or the Lower Brahmaputra from that of the Tibetan Sangpo or Upper Brahmaputra which rises not far from the sources of the Sutlej. Mount Everest (29,002 feet), the highest known mountain in the world, and Kanchinjunga (27,813 feet) the third highest, the former in Nepal, the latter on the borders of Nepal and Sikkim, are the two most prominent mountains in this line of peaks. Chumalari (23,944 feet) lies farther east in Bhotan.

The highlands of South Behar and Chutia Nágpur are the eastern end of the belt of hilly country already noticed at p. 15, as stretching across India from the Gulf of Cambay. They include no definite mountain range. They are a table-land, in places more than 2000 feet above the sea, in which the rivers have cut their valleys more or less deeply, and with local rounded or flat-topped hills rising 2000 feet and more above the plateau. One group, the Rajmehal hills, occupies the angle between the Behar plain and the delta. Another broken line of hills bearing various local names runs across south-east Behar. The highest hill in western Bengal is Parasnáth (4481 feet), the summit of which is a place of pilgrimage very sacred to the Jain sect. In the extreme west of Chutia Nágpur the table-land of Main Pát, 50 miles long by 40 broad, and surrounded by a steep escarpment, rises to 3700 feet above the sea.

The hills east of the Gangetic delta are very different. They consist of long steep parallel ridges running north and south, the rivers in narrow valleys between them. The highest range is about 80 miles from the coast, and its highest points, Sang Al Klang and Malselai Mon or Blue Mountain, are respectively 7438 and 7100 feet above the sea.

The three largest rivers of Bengal are the Ganges, the Brahmaputra, and the Megna; the last was formerly the main stream of the Brahmaputra, but its upper part now receives only the drainage of Sylhet and Cachar.

The Ganges enters Bengal from the North-West Provinces at Chupra, where it is joined by the Gogra, as already noticed at p. 74. Above this junction as far as the Karamnása (Karmnása), it flows between Bengal on the south and the North-West Provinces on the north bank. A few miles farther down it receives two large tributaries, viz. the Soane (Són) from Central India, and the Gunduk (Gandak) from the Himalaya, the first just above Dinapore, the second opposite Patna. Farther on, a little below Monghyr, it is joined by the united waters of the Bur Gunduk and Bágh-mati, and again, below Bhágalpur, by those of the Ghagri and Koosee, all Himalayan rivers. About 20 miles below this junction it sweeps round the end of the Rajmehal hills, and its course, which has hitherto been nearly east, changes to south-east. Twenty miles farther down it gives off its first deltaic branch the Bhagiruthee, and this, uniting with two lower branches, the Jelinghee and the Matabhanga, forms the Hooghly, which flows past Calcutta; and recruited by several rivers from the table-land to the west, enters the sea through a broad estuary at Saugor Point. Below the head of the delta the main stream takes the name of the Pudda (*Padma*, a lotus); one more river, the Maha-nuddy, from the Sikkim Himalaya, enters it on the north, and finally it unites with the Brahmaputra at Goalundo.

The Gogra river has already been noticed under the North-West Provinces, and the Soane (Són) is chiefly in Central India, and will be described under that province. The Gunduk, an equally large river, drains both the northern and southern slopes of about 100 miles of the Himalaya, between the great peak of Dhaulagiri and Kathmándu the capital of Nepal. Three streams, the Kali Gunduk, the Buria Gunduk, and the Trisul Gunduk, which have their origin in Tibet within a few miles of the Sangpo, and sepa-rately break through the great snowy range, unite in the Lower Himalaya, and as the Gunduk issue through the outer range. Then turning to the south-east, the great river crosses northern Behar as a navigable stream, and enters the Ganges opposite Patna.

The next stream of chief importance is the Koosee, which also rises in Tibet far to the north of the snowy range, and receives the whole drainage of the Himalaya from Kathmándu eastward to Kanchinjunga, a distance of 90 miles. Its subsequent course is due south across the plain. All the other northern tributaries of the Ganges in Bengal rise on the southern face of the great snowy range.

The Brahmaputra enters Bengal from Assam at its north-east corner, flowing due south. After receiving one or two tributaries from Bhotan, and the Teesta or Pagla from Sikkim, it continues its southward course to its junction with the Ganges. From the Gáro hills to its junction with the Nugna it takes the name of the Jamoona.

The Teesta, which drains the whole of Sikkim, rises far to the north of the snowy range, which it crosses to the east of Kanchinjunga, and issues on the plains below Darjiling. Up to 1787 it flowed southward to the Ganges at Jaffirganj, but in that year it changed its course to the south-east across the plain of northern Bengal, and under the name of the Pagla it joins the Brahmaputra opposite the Gáro hills.

The Megna, which up to the end of the last century was the main stream of the Brahmaputra, is now fed by the Surmá and the Barák from Sylhet and Cachar, and receives water from the Brahmaputra only when that river is in flood. It joins the Jamoona just within the Tropic of Cancer, and the united waters of the three great rivers are poured out to sea through the Megna channel, near the eastern margin of the delta.

Most of the rivers of the western plateau flow eastward. The chief of them are the Adjai, the Damoodur, and the Roopnarayan, which unite with the Hooghly or its estuary; the Subanrika, the Baitarni, and the Brahmini, which discharge into the Bay of Bengal. The Mahanuddy (Mahánadi), a very large river, enters Orissa from the Central Provinces, and together with the Brahmini forms a delta that projects into the Bay of Bengal, terminating at Point Palmiras.

Administrative Divisions.—The province of Bengal,

in the more extended sense of the term, consists of nine divisions, five of which are included in Bengal proper, two in Behar, one in Orissa, and one in Chutia Nágpur. These are subdivided into districts as follow :—

Divisions.	Districts.	Area. Sq. m.	Population.
Patna	Patna	2,079	1,756,856
	Gya	4,712	2,124,682
	Shahabad	4,365	1,964,909
	Mozufferpore	3,003	2,582,060
	Durbhunga	3,335	2,633,447
	Sarun	2,622	2,280,382
	Champarun	3,531	1,721,608
Bhágalpur	Monghyr	3,921	1,969,774
	Bhágalpur	4,268	1,966,158
	Purneah	4,956	1,848,687
	Maldah	1,891	710,448
	Sonthal Pergunnahs	5,456	1,568,093
Rajshahye	Dinagepore	4,118	1,514,346
	Rajshahye	2,361	1,338,638
	Rungpore	3,486	2,097,964
	Bogra	1,498	734,358
	Pubna	1,847	1,311,728
	Darjiling	1,234	155,179
	Jalpáiguri	2,884	581,562
Burdwan	Burdwan	2,697	1,391,823
	Bankoora	2,621	1,041,752
	Beerbhoom	1,756	794,428
	Midnapore	5,082	2,517,802
	Hooghly	1,223	1,012,768
	Howrah	476	635,381
Presidency	24 Pergunnahs	2,097	1,618,420
	Calcutta	8	433,219
	,, suburbs	23	251,439
	Nuddea	3,404	2,017,847
	Jessore	2,276	1,577,249
	Khoolna	2,077	1,079,948
	Moorshedabad	2,144	1,226,790
Dacca	Dacca	2,797	2,116,350
	Furreedpore	2,267	1,631,734
	Backergunge	3,649	1,900,889
	Mymensingh	6,287	3,051,966
Chittagong	Chittagong	2,567	1,132,341
	Noakholly	1,641	820,772
	Tipperah	2,491	1,519,338
	Hill Tracts	5,419	101,597

Divisions.	Districts.	Area. Sq. m.	Population.
Orissa	Cuttack	3,517	1,738,165
	Pooree	2,473	888,487
	Balasore	2,066	945,280
	Angul	881	101,903
	Banki	116	56,900
Chutia Nágpur	Hazáribágh	7,021	1,104,742
	Lohardugga	12,045	1,609,244
	Singhbhoom	3,753	453,775
	Manbhoom	4,147	1,058,228

The most westerly division is that of Patna, bordering on the North-West Provinces. Four districts, Sarun, Chumparun, Mozufferpore, and Durbhunga, are on the plain north of the Ganges, the remaining three to the south of that river. The Bhágalpur division follows it on the east; Purneah and Maldah being wholly to the north or east of the river, Monghyr and Bhágalpur districts on both sides, and the Sonthal Pergunnahs in the upland country to the south. These two divisions constitute Behar.

The Rajshahye division occupies the northern plain between Behar, the Ganges, and the Brahmaputra and the Darjiling hills; the Burdwan division the south-western margin of the delta and the adjacent slope of the uplands, bounded on the east by the Hooghly. The Presidency division comprises the whole of the delta between the Hooghly and the Madhumati rivers and a small strip to the west of the Bhagiruthee. In the Dacca division the districts of Mymensingh and Dacca lie between the Jamoona and the Surmá and Megna; those of Furreedpore and Burrisal between the Madhumati and the Ganges and Megna estuary. The Chittagong division is wholly to the east of the Megna, including the eastern margin of the delta and the adjacent hill country. These five divisions make up Bengal proper.

The Orissa division consists of the coast plain along the north-west corner of the bay and the hills to the west up to the border of the Central Provinces. And Chutia Nágpur comprises the whole of the hill country west of the Burdwan division and south of Behar, as far west as the Central Provinces and the state of Rewah in Central India.

Native States.—The most important native states feudatory to Bengal are Cooch Behar (1307 square miles), in the north-east corner of the province, and Hill Tipperah (4086 square miles), which consists of the northern portion of the hill tract east of the delta. All the remaining states are small tracts of hill and jungle in the west of the Orissa division and in the south of Chutia Nágpur. The former of these are termed the Tributary Mehals of Orissa, and cover 15,187 square miles, the latter the Garhját states, occupying 16,054 square miles.

The City of Calcutta.—Calcutta (Fig. 12), founded by Job Charnock in 1686, is not only the capital of Bengal, but, as the winter residence of the viceroy and the permanent seat of the offices of the supreme Government, also the capital of British India. Before the construction of railways and the Suez Canal it was by far the most important seat of trade. The Ganges, which was then the great highway for inland traffic, brought down to it nearly the whole trade of northern India, and especially the produce of the Gangetic plain, the most productive portion of India. Its commerce has increased steadily up to the present time, but less rapidly than that of Bombay, which has superior advantages in a magnificent harbour and greater proximity to Europe; and notwithstanding the possession of a broad river and docks, Calcutta now holds only the second place as an emporium of foreign trade. It is the seat of a university, a splendid museum, a zoological and a botanic garden and herbarium, and of the oldest scientific society in Asia, the Asiatic Society of Bengal; as a centre of intellectual activity and European science it still ranks first among eastern cities. Including the suburb of Howrah, its population in 1881 amounted to nearly 800,000. It is situated on the eastern bank of the Hooghly, 86 miles from the sea, in lat. 22° 33′ E. and long. 88° 23′ N., about 16 feet only above sea-level. To the east is the salt water lake, an unfilled depression of the delta, communicating by a canal with the river, and in the opposite direction with the creeks of the Sunderbuns. The suburb of Howrah, on the opposite bank of the river, is connected with Calcutta by a large floating bridge.

Fig. 12.—Calcutta from the Ouchterlony Monument, looking north-west.

Other Towns in Bengal.—Next to Calcutta, Patna (170,000) is the largest town in the province, situated on the right bank of the Ganges, below the confluence of the Soane river. All the opium produced in Bengal is manufactured at the Government factory at this place.

Other places of importance are—Dacca (79,000) on the Buriganga, the capital of Bengal under the Delhi emperors in the seventeenth century, and its chief port before the rise of Calcutta; famous for the fine texture of its muslins. Moorshedabad (39,000), on the Bhagiruthee, the capital of the Muhammadan rulers of Bengal in the eighteenth century. Hooghly and Chinsurah, now one town (31,000), on the right bank of the Hooghly, 25 miles above Calcutta; the former founded by the Portuguese, the latter by the Dutch, but both now British. Chandernagore (23,000), a few miles lower down on the same side of the river, a French possession, the only one in Bengal; the territory covers three square miles. Cuttack (42,000), the chief town of Orissa, at the head of the Mahanuddy (Mahánadi) delta, well known for its filagree silver work. The town of Pooree (22,000) on the coast, 50 miles south of Cuttack, is the site of the famous pagoda of Jaganáth, one of the chief places of Hindu pilgrimage. Chittagong (21,000) on the Karnaphuli river, three miles inland from the coast of the bay, opposite the mouth of the Megna channel, a nest of piracy in the seventeenth century, and now a port of some importance. A railway is being constructed to Cachar and Upper Assam, and when finished it may be expected that the trade of Chittagong will be much increased. There are several tea-gardens in the neighbourhood. Gya (76,000), in south Behar. In its neighbourhood is the famous temple of Budh Gya, commemorating the spot where Sakya Muni (Siddhárta or Gautama) attained Buddhahood in the sixth century B.C.; also the site of the great Buddhist monastery of Nalanda.

The only hill-station in Bengal is Darjiling (6500 to 7000 feet), on the crest of a ridge of the Sikkim Himalaya, sixteen miles from the plains, now reached by a railway. The tea-gardens on the lower hills and on the slope at their foot produce some of the finest teas of India. In the same neighbourhood is also the chief cinchona plantation of the Government. Forty miles to the north rises the great peak of Kanchinjunga, one of the grandest mountains in the world.

Population.—In 1881 the population of Bengal was 69,536,861, of which 3 millions are that of native states. This gives a general average for the whole province of 362 souls to the square mile. In the Patna division alone there are 524 to the square mile, and in its three most populous districts 860 to the square mile. This is more than half as many again as in Belgium, the most densely-peopled state in Europe.

There are upwards of 2 millions of aboriginals, chiefly in Chutia Nágpur and south Behar; of the remainder, about two-thirds are Hindus and one-third Muhammadans. These last are most numerous in northern and eastern Bengal, where they form from 75 to 80 per cent of the inhabitants.

Only the people of Bengal proper are termed Bengalis; those of Behar are Beharis; and those of Orissa, Ooryahs. Each of these have their own language, all chiefly derived from Prakrit.

Productions.—Bengal is richer than any other province in coalfields, the most important of which are in the valley of the Damoodur to the west of Calcutta. Iron ores are abundant, and are smelted by the English process at some works now in possession of the Government. Copper is mined to some extent in Chutia Nágpur.

As in other parts of India, the chief produce of the province is agricultural. The most important staples are rice, pulses, tea, indigo, opium, betel nut, pepper, cinchona, jute, cotton, silk, and tobacco. Shell-lac and lac dye and tusseh silk are collected in the forests of Chutia Nágpur.

The principal manufactures are cotton cloths and gunny bags, which are largely exported for packing grain.

Railways.—From Calcutta two systems of railways start on opposite sides of the Hooghly, and are now connected by a railway bridge at Hooghly, 24 miles above Calcutta. The main line of the East Indian Railway starting from Howrah on the right bank, passes through Serampore,

Chandernagore, and Hooghly, and then strikes north-west to Burdwan, Ráníganj with its coal-mines, and across the plateau of the Sonthal country to the Ganges at Mokameh. Thence it follows the river to Patna and Buxar, and leaves the province at the Karamnása on its way to Benares and North-Western India. A loop line from near Burdwan runs north to the Ganges at Rajmehal, and thence follows up the river through Bhágalpur to rejoin the main line at Luckiserai. Several short branches connect these lines with neighbouring places, viz. Rájmehal, Monghyr, and the coal-mines around Barackur. Longer branches lead to Turkessur (a great place of pilgrimage), Moorshedabad, the coal-mines of Kurhurbari, and from Patna to Gya; from Asansol beyond Ráníganj, leads off the future trunk line to Nágpur and Bombay, which is now under construction, and is destined to open out the extensive coalfields of Chutia Nágpur.

The system on the left bank of the Hooghly consists of railways to Diamond harbour on the Hooghly estuary below Calcutta, to Port Canning on the Mutlah river, and two lines northward, one direct to Jessore, the other to the Ganges, which one branch follows down to Goalundo, the starting-place for steamers to Dacca, Cachar, and Assam. The other branch communicates by a steam ferry with the terminus of the Northern Bengal Railway on the northern bank of the river. This railway system consists, first, of a line due north to Darjiling; second, of a branch from this eastward to the Brahmaputra below Dhubri, whence mail steamers proceed up the river to Assam; third, a branch westward to Dinagepore, which is being extended to connect it with the Tirhoot railway system. This last starts from the Ganges opposite Mokameh (on the East Indian Railway); one branch proceeds to Durbhunga and then north and east to the Koosee river; another to Mozufferpore and on to Motiharee and Bettiah in the north-western corner of Behar; and from Mozufferpore a third runs to the Ganges opposite Patna. Lastly, the North-Western Railway, starting from the same point opposite Patna, runs north-west to Gorakhpur and the bank of the Gogra opposite Fyzabad, which is on the Oudh and Rohilkand

Railway. The Ganges has not been bridged below Benares.

In eastern Bengal a railway runs from Narainganj, the port of Dacca, northward to Mymensingh, and another is being constructed to bring Assam and Cachar into communication with the port of Chittagong.

Assam

Area, 46,341 square miles. Population, 4,881,426

Name and Government.—The ancient kingdom of Assam (from Ahom, the name of a former ruling race) included only the valley of the Brahmaputra from where the river issues from the Himalaya to where it enters on the plains of Bengal. When, in 1874, Assam was constituted a distinct province of the empire, there were added to it the valley of Cachar and the plain of Sylhet, together with the intervening hills, the whole now forming a chief commissionership, with the seat of Government at Shillong on the Khási hills.

General Features.—The Assam valley proper is 450 miles long and averages 50 in width, bounded on the north by the Himalaya, on the south-east by the Pátkai range, which with the hills beyond separate it from Upper Burma, and on the south-west by a branching mass of hills, sections of which are called after the aboriginal tribes that occupy them, the Nágá, Jaintía, Khási and Gáro hills. These separate it from Cachar and Sylhet. The valley is obstructed midway by the Mikir hills, which divide it into Upper and Lower Assam. Upper Assam is still mainly either forest or marsh covered with gigantic grass; the latter to a width of from six to twenty miles on the borders of the river, the former on the higher ground and the adjacent hills. The marsh land when cleared is converted into rice-fields, and tea-gardens are established in clearings in the forest, but these are of insignificant extent in proportion to the unreclaimed land.

The Sylhet plain, to the south of the Gáro and Khási hills, is broader and shorter, bounded on the south by the hills of Tipperah. It is traversed by the two branches of the Barák river which enters it from Cachar, and much of the intervening flat consists of swamps termed *bíls*, which in the rainy season are deeply submerged. Nevertheless, much of this submerged land is planted with a peculiar variety of rice which grows as the water rises, sometimes to a length of 12 feet. Tea-gardens are established on the hillocks termed *tílas* around the plain, and orange plantations on the slopes of the Khási hills. Cachar is the valley of the Barák. It is intersected by long ridges of low hills that run northward from the Lushai hills on its southern border, and the depressions between them are also marshes, covered with extensive sheets of water in the rains. Tea-gardens and villages are established on the higher ground round their margins and on the *tílas* or low hills.

The Gáro and Khási hills form an undulating and hilly table-land from 2000 to 6000 feet above the sea, rising abruptly from the plain of Sylhet, culminating in the Shillong ridge and declining gradually to the valley of Assam. The surface is chiefly grassy, being kept clear of forest by the annual burning of the grass ; but forest clothes the sides and bottoms of the deep valleys and ravines cut by the drainage. These hills and also those on the border of Upper Assam include several small coalfields.

The climate of the province is damp at all times of the year. The rainfall is heavy, and falls in eight or nine months of the year ; and neither is the summer very hot nor the winter very cold, but in the latter season fogs are very prevalent. The vegetation is luxuriant and tropical in character, although no part of the province lies within the tropic. Elephants, rhinosceroses, buffaloes, and many other large animals abound in the jungles, and many kinds are met with that do not occur in other parts of India, such as the *mithan* or *gayal*, a large kind of cattle, commonly domesticated by the hillmen, and the *hoolock*, a species of gibbon. Birds, reptiles, insects, and land mollusca are also very varied and abundant.

Area and Position.—The province extends over 46,341 square miles, of which total the Assam valley occupies 21,414, the plains of Cachar and Sylhet 6725, and the remainder is hill country. Its most northerly point is in

N. lat. 28° 20′, its most southerly in 23° 57′, therefore just outside the tropic, and it extends between the meridians of 89° 44′ and 97° 8′ E. long. Its greatest length from nearly east to west is 450 miles, and its extreme width 200 miles. It is bounded on the north by the state of Bhotan, and by hills occupied by a number of independent hill tribes, the Akas, Daphlas, Miris, Lukotias, and Mishmis, succeeding each other in the above order from west to east. On the east of the Assam valley the hills are similarly possessed by the Kamptis, and on the south-east by the Singphos or Kachins. Farther south the province is bounded by Manipur, the Lushai hills, and Hill Tipperah, and on the west by Bengal.

Mountains and Rivers.—The Himalaya bounds the province on the north, receding to the north-east in the upper part of Assam. The great snowy range comes to an end in about the 93d meridian, terminating in a series of great peaks between 21,500 and 22,800 feet in height; but the Tibetan snowy range continues eastwards with peaks not exceeding 16,700 feet in height, interrupted, however, by the great rivers that come down from Tibet. At its north-eastern extremity, the Assam valley is shut in by high ranges running southward from the eastern Himalaya, which, together with other parallel ranges beyond, are the origin of the great meridianal system of Burma and Siam. From these the Pátkai range, which bounds the Brahmaputra valley on the south, branches off to the west and south-west, and farther down gives off the Barail range, which divides Assam and Cachar from Manipur. One great spur of this range runs off westward to the north of the Barák valley, dividing it from that of the Dhansiri, and unites with the Nágá and Jaintía hills. These, and the Khási and Gáro hills beyond, have a general east and west direction, separating Lower Assam from Sylhet. To the south of Cachar the Lushai hills, and to the south of Sylhet the hills of Tipperah, all consisting of parallel north and south ridges, run southwards into western Burma and Arakan.

The Brahmaputra (Son of Brahma) river runs the whole length of the Assam valley. Of the rivers from the mountains that contribute to it, it is now known that the chief feeder is that which rises a little to the east of Manasorawar lake; under various local names, of which the best known is the Sangpo, runs eastward through Tibet across 12° of longitude, and then, after a great bend to the north, turning southwards, breaks through the Himalaya round the extremity of the great snowy range, and enters Upper Assam as the Dihang river. At Sadiya this joins a smaller river from the east, which has hitherto borne the name of the Lohit Brahmaputra, and enters Assam at the Brahmakund, a sacred pool, 2000 feet above the sea. Its source is probably in the north of the Zayul district of Tibet, in about N. lat. 29°, and it receives the drainage of the whole of that district, from which its course has been traced westwards through the mountains to the Brahmakund. A third river, the Dibang, from the north, probably identical with the Kenpu of Eastern Tibet, joins the Dihang just above the confluence. In its course through Assam the Brahmaputra receives a number of tributaries both from north and south. Of the former, the largest in addition to those just mentioned, are the Subansiri, which drains a very extensive tract of the Himalaya around the eastern end of the great snowy range, and the Manas from central Bhotan, joining the Brahmaputra opposite Gauháti. On the south the Noa Dihing, and the Dihing and Dikhu from the Pátkai range, the Dhansiri from the same and the Barail and Nágá hills, and the Kalang from the Nágá, Jaintía, and Mikir hills.

Cachar is traversed by the Barák, which enters it from Manipur, after a tortuous course round the Barail range. It receives the Sonai and the Dhaleswari from the Lushai hills, and on entering Sylhet divides into two branches. The northern takes the name of the Surmá, receives the heavy drainage of the south face of the Jaintía, Khási, and Gáro hills, and then turning southwards enters the Megna. The southern branch, called the Kusiyára, receives some small rivers from the Tipperah hills, and also unites with the Megna.

Administrative Divisions.—The Assam province is divided into districts as follow:—

Divisions.	Districts.	Area. Sq. m.	Population.
Hills	Gáro hills	3180	85,634
	Khási and Jaintía hills	6157	169,360
	Nágá hills	6400 ?	94,380
	Cachar hill tracts	2465	24,433
Surmá valley	Sylhet	5440	1,969,009
	Cachar	1285	289,425
Assam valley	Gáro hills, plains	473	23,914
	Goalpára	3897	446,232
	Kámrúp	3631	644,960
	Darrang	3418	273,333
	Nowgong	3417	310,579
	Sibságar	2855	370,274
	Lakhimpur	3723	179,893

In Assam proper, Lakhimpur and Sibságar divide Upper Assam between them, the former to the north of the Brahmaputra and Noa Dihing, the latter to the south. In the central part of the valley, Darrang is the plain north of the river and Nowgong that on the south; and in Lower Assam, Kámrúp and Goalpára extend on both sides of the Brahmaputra. A small tract of the Gáro hill district is also on the plain.

The eastern half of the hill country south of Sibságar is occupied by Nágá tribes (see Fig. 4.); the Khási and Jaintía hills lie south of the central part of the valley, and the Gáro hills are to the west, in the angle formed by the southern bend of the Brahmaputra.

To the south of the hills Cachar occupies the eastern part of the Barák valley and the surrounding hills, and Sylhet the western plain, traversed by the two branches of the river.

Native Territory.—There are no native states properly so called in the province of Assam, but two tracts are occupied by native tribes but partially or indirectly ruled by the British Government. These are the Khási and Jaintía hills, and the Singpho territory already noticed at p. 96. To the east of Cachar is the native state of Manipur, under the protection of the British Government. It is a valley surrounded by hills, which include the upper waters of the Barák and those of the Nam Kathen, the main feeder of the Myittha, a tributary of the Chindwin, which is itself an affluent of the Irawadi.

Towns.—There is no town in the province containing more than 18,000 inhabitants. In the Assam valley the most important places are Gauháti (12,000) in Kámrúp, on the south bank of the Brahmaputra; and Sibságar and Dibrugarh, the centres of the tea industry in Upper Assam. The seat of government is at Shillong, on the Khási hills, 5000 feet above the sea. Thirty miles to the south of it is Cherra Poonjee, the wettest known place in the world, with an annual average rainfall of 473 inches, and sometimes over 600 inches in the year. Sylhet, on the Surmá river (18,000), is the largest town in the province, and Silchar, on the Barák, is the centre of the tea plantations in Cachar. It is much subject to earthquakes.

Population.—The population of the province in 1881, as far as it could be enumerated, was 4,881,426, giving a general average of 105 to the square mile. The total population of the hill districts was only 374,000, or about 20 to the square mile. The people of the Assam valley and Cachar are for the most part of Indo-Chinese races, more or less allied to those of the hills around, but of late years there has been much immigration from Bengal to supply labour for the tea-gardens. The people of Sylhet are more akin to those of Eastern Bengal.

On the central hills are Gáros, Khásis, and Nágás. The last are but little civilised, and their different clans, distinguished by the patterns tattooed on their faces, are generally inimical to each other. The Singphos of the Pátkai hills are a more peaceable race. But the Lushais of the hills south of Cachar resemble the Nágás in their predatory habits, and from time to time raid on each other or on the inhabitants of the border plains.

Productions.—Coal is worked in the Khási hills and in Upper Assam. Petroleum is also known to occur there. Small quantities of gold are obtained from the rivers, and limestone is quarried in Sylhet for the supply of Bengal. The forests produce sál, sissu, ironwood, and some other excellent timbers, also bamboos and rattans; and india-rubber and tusseh silk are collected by the hillmen. Sylhet grows rice for exportation, but the Assam valley and Cachar do not raise sufficient grain for the wants of their inhabitants. The great staple product of the province is tea, the plantations of which in 1887 amounted to 234,000 acres. Other articles of export are betel nut, mustard seed, and oranges. Silk and cotton cloth, grass mats, and several articles of less importance are manufactured on a small scale.

Railways and Steamer Lines.—There is at present a small railway in Upper Assam, from Dibrugarh to the bank of the Brahmaputra opposite Sadiya, with a branch to the coal-mines of Makum. Also a short line of 7½ miles down the south face of the Khási hills, from Cherra Poonjee to Company Ganj. Otherwise, the chief means of communication are the river steamers, which navigate the Brahmaputra regularly up to Dibrugarh, and bring down to Calcutta the teas of the province. The mail steamers start from the terminus of the Northern Bengal Railway, a few miles below Dhubri. In Cachar, in the rainy season, steamers ascend the Barák to Silchar, but in the dry season only as far as Chattack, twelve miles below Sylhet, on the Surmá, and to Fenchuganj, on the Kusiyára. A line of railway is now under construction from Chittagong on the coast of Bengal to Cachar, and through the hills of Asálu and down the Dhansiri valley to Upper Assam. A good road leads across the Khási hills from Goalpára through Shillong and Cherra Poonjee to Teria Ghat, not far from Sylhet.

Rájputána

Area, 132,461 square miles. Population, 10,729,114

Name and Government.—Rájputána (the country of the Rájputs or sons of rulers), or Rájasthán (the country of rulers), is a generally arid tract of North-Western India divided between twenty native states and one British district. Seventeen of these states are ruled by Rájput (Hindu) princes, a warlike race of ancient descent (see Fig. 13), who at one time ruled the whole of Northern India, but were driven out or superseded by the early Muhammadan invaders. The government of these states is of a simple patriarchal rather than feudal character, the lands of each being parcelled out between the Rajah and the members of his clan, each of whom, at least in the western states, rules his own little domain, paying certain dues, and contributing military service to the chief of the state.

General Features.—The Rájput states occupy the greater part of the so-called desert tract between the Indus and the Arvalis; also a portion of the table-land east of the Arvalis. The former is a great plain, either rocky or covered with sand-hills, some of which are as much as 500 feet in height. This part is known as the *Thar.* About Jeysulmere, and again in the east, in the neighbourhood of the Arvalis, are some rocky hills, most of which rise only 200 or 300 feet above the plain. Very much of the surface is covered with a dry scrub, with a few small trees. In other parts the soil is salt and barren. Except the Luni, the waters of which are salt, there are no rivers, and water is obtained from wells of great depth.

This plain extends up to the Arvali range, which forms the western boundary of the Málwa table-land. This range runs from the neighbourhood of Delhi for about 400 miles to the south-west, terminating opposite to Mount Abu. The northern half, from Delhi to Jeypore, is the mere skeleton of a range, and consists of an interrupted series of low parallel rocky ridges, two or three miles apart, rising from a sandy plain which slopes away gently to the north-west and south-east; but from Ajmere southwards the range is continuous, with a greater fall to the west than to the east, in some places as much as 1500 feet, and the country being damper, many parts of the hills are covered with forest.

Of the table-land east of the Arvalis, the northern part is a sandy plain, crossed at intervals by low ridges of sandstone, and most of the ground is cultivated. The south-western part consists of plains of fertile black soil interspersed with flat-topped hills of volcanic rock, similar to those that cover an enormous extent of country in the north-west of the peninsula. There are numerous artificial lakes, and many rivers; the hills are clad with forest, and the plains richly cultivated. The wilder parts of this region are occupied by aboriginal tribes.

Position and Area.—Rájputána occupies a total area of 132,461 miles, of which only 2711 are directly administered by officers of the British Government. It extends between 30° 12′ and 22° 59′ N. lat., a distance of 580 miles; and between 69° 30′ and 78° 13′ E. long., a distance of 480 miles. It is surrounded on the north-east by the Punjab and North-West Provinces, on the north-west by the native state of Baháwalpur, feudatory to the Punjab, on the south-west by Sind, on the south by Guzerat, and on the south-east and east by the native states of Málwa and Gwalior, which are included in the Central India Agency.

Hills and Rivers.—There are no elevations deserving the name of mountains in Rájputána. The chief hill ranges are the Arvalis already noticed, nowhere rising to 3000 feet, and the Meywar and Málwa Ghats, which run off to the south-east, from the southern end of the Arvalis, bounding the plateau on the south-west as far as the Nerbudda. Some isolated hills rise from the plain to the west of the range; the highest, Mount Abu (5650 feet), is crowned with a Jain temple, much frequented as a place of pilgrimage by the adherents of that sect. The Boondee hills on the plateau, 70 miles east of the Arvalis, between the Banás and Chambal rivers, rise to 1793 feet.

The plain of western Rájputána is almost devoid of rivers owing to the scantiness of the rainfall, which diminishes from 20 inches on the Arvalis to no more than 6 inches in the extreme west. The only stream of importance is the Luni (salt river), which rises in the Arvalis near Ajmere, receives the drainage of the western face of the southern half of the range, and discharges itself into the Gulf of Cutch. Except occasionally after heavy rain its waters are very salt.

The Rájputána table-land east of the Arvalis is drained by the Chambal and its tributary the Banás. The Banás rises in the hills of Meywar, flows to the north-east past the famous fortress of Chítor, skirts the Boondee hills, and after a course of 300 miles joins the

Chambal. The Chambal, the largest river in Rájputána, rises in the Vindhyan Ghats of Málwa, not far from Indore, enters the province at Chaurasgarh, skirts the eastern flank of the Boondee hills, receives the Banás as well as several large streams from the south-east, and for 130 miles separates Rájputána from Central India. Below Dholpur it turns eastward, leaving the province and forming the boundary of Central India and the North-West Provinces for 60 miles, and soon afterwards falls into the Jumna. It has a total course of 560 miles.

The southern extremity of the Arvalis and the hills of Meywar, and some of the small states in the extreme south, are drained by the headwaters of the Sábarmati and the Mahi, both of which rivers flow southwards into the Gulf of Cambay.

The Sámbhar lake is a shallow salt lake immediately west of the Arvalis, a few miles from Jeypore. Like other salt lakes it has no outlet, but receives the scanty drainage of about 90 miles of the Arvalis north of Ajmere, and increases or shrinks according to the supply and the evaporation, sometimes extending to a length of 20 miles, and sometimes nearly drying up; 40,000 tons of salt are manufactured annually from its waters.

Administrative Divisions and Native States.—The British district of Ajmere-Merwara is situated in and around a high part of the Arvalis in the heart of the province. It covers an area of 2711 square miles, the greater part of which is hill country.

The largest of the twenty native states are Jodhpore, Bickaneer, Jeysulmere, Jeypore, and Oodeypore, each of which exceeds 10,000 square miles of area. The remainder are all under 4000 square miles. Bickaneer occupies all the northern, Jeysulmere the western, and Jodhpore the southern and south-eastern portion of the desert tract to the north-west of the Arvalis. Jeypore occupies most of the eastern portion, and extends also to the eastern plateau. Oodeypore or Meywar lies wholly on a hilly part of the table-land at the southern end of the chain. The Rána or ruler of this state is the head of the Sesodia clan, the oldest and purest of the Rájput race, and has the most ancient lineage of any existing sovereign house, being a descendant of the semi-mythical hero Ráma, now worshipped as an incarnation of Vishnu.

The areas and population of the native states are as follow :—

State.	Area. Sq. m.	Population.	State.	Area. Sq. m.	Population.
Jodhpore	37,000	1,750,403	Ulwur	3,024	682,926
Bickaneer	22,340	509,021	Sirohee	3,020	142,903
Jeysulmere	16,447	108,143	Jhallawar	2,694	340,488
Jeypore	14,465	2,534,357	Tonk	2,509	338,029
Oodeypore	12,670	1,494,220	Boondee	2,300	254,701
Kotah	3,797	517,275	Other states	9,484	1,575,926

Towns.—The chief town of the province is Ajmere. From the time of the early Muhammadan emperors it has been held, except for short intervals, by the power paramount in Rájputána, and is now the residence of the Governor-General's agent for the province. On a lofty hill (2855 feet) immediately overlooking the town is the fortress of Táragarh. Nusseerabad, the chief military cantonment in Rájputána, is fourteen miles south of Ajmere. Abu on the hill of the same name (3945 feet), in the state of Sirohee, is the summer residence of the Governor-General's agent, and also a sanitarium for Rájputána and the neighbouring Bombay province of Guzerat.

Jeypore, the capital of the state of the same name, 80 miles north-east of Ajmere, is a handsome modern walled city, founded by Jai Singh, a former Rajah of the state and a famous astronomer, who removed his capital from Amber, now deserted and in ruins, in 1728. The lofty masonry structures erected for astronomical observations are still to be seen at the palace. Oodeypore, also the capital of the state so named, picturesquely situated on a ridge overlooking a great artificial lake. Bickaneer and Jodhpore, in the western desert, are also the capitals of their respective states, and the residence of many rich Hindu bankers, mostly of the Jain sect. Both these are strongly walled cities.

Population.—The population of Rájputána in 1881 was nearly 461,000 in British territory and upwards of

$10\frac{1}{4}$ millions in the native states, averaging 170 to the square mile in the former and 79 in the latter. That of Jeysulmere, in the heart of the desert tract, is only between six and seven to the square mile. About seven-eighths are Hindus and one-twelfth Muhammadans. The Jains, chiefly money-dealers and merchants, are more numerous than in most other Indian provinces.

FIG. 13.—RÁJPUTS.

In respect of caste, the Rájputs (Fig. 13), who are the chief landowners, number less than 5 per cent of the population. Brahmans are nearly twice as numerous, and the Mahájans, or money-dealers, and the low caste Chamárs (hide and leather workers) also exceed them in number; while Minás (originally a lawless caste, recruited from the outcasts and adventurers of various castes), Gujárs (herdsmen), and Jats, are respectively nearly equal in number to the Rájputs. The aboriginal Bhíls, more or less Hinduised, form about 1 per cent of the population, and those who still adhere to the wild life of their forefathers are estimated at about half as many again. They occupy the southern Arvalis and the hill tracts of Meywar.

Productions.—Salt is manufactured not only at the Sámbhar lake but also in salt tracts around the Luni. The hills of the Arvali chain yield the only cobalt ores found in India (not including Nepal), also copper and iron ores, and alum shale. The white marble and fine red sandstone used in the beautiful buildings of Agra and Delhi come from north-eastern Rájputána.

Owing to the scantiness of the rainfall the greater part of Rájputána is agriculturally poor. In the western states especially the produce of the small cultivated tracts is precarious, and only in the eastern and southern states are two crops obtained annually. But the so-called desert tract affords fodder for enormous herds of camels, cattle, sheep, and goats.

Railways.—The Rájputána State Railway, on the narrow gauge, starts from Delhi and Agra, the two branches meeting at Bandikoi, south of Ulwur. Thence it runs westward to Jeypore, and skirting the eastern flank of the Arvalis to Ajmere. Here it divides; the western branch crosses the Arvalis, and runs south-west past Mount Abu into Guzerat, where it meets the Bombay and Baroda Railway at Ahmedabad. This is the mail route between the Punjab and Bombay. The eastern branch runs through Nusseerabad, Neemuch, and Indore, and descending a ghat through the Vindhyan range, and crossing the Nerbudda, terminates at Khandwa on the Great Peninsular Railway. A small branch from near Jeypore leads to the Sámbhar salt lake, and a branch from the western line runs to Jodhpore, and to the salt works at Pachpadra on the Luni river.

Central India Agency

Area, 75,079 square miles. Population, 9,261,907

Name and Government.—The territory thus denominated is, like Rájputána, a congeries of native states, under the general superintendence of an agent of the Governor-

General, and must not be confounded with the Central Provinces, which lie immediately to the south-east, and are for the most part directly administered by British officials. It includes the large states of Gwalior and Indore, under the Maráthá (Hindu) houses of Sindia and Holkar; of Bhopál, ruled by a Muhammadan lady of Pathán (Afghan) descent, and Rewah, the chief of which is of Rájput race. Besides these there are 78 petty states, varying from a few square miles only up to between 2000 and 3000 square miles. The ruling families of most of these are of Rájput stock, a few only being either Maráthá or Muhammadan, and many of the smaller states are feudatory to the larger states either of this agency or those of Rájputána. The whole are classified in nine groups, each under an officer termed the Political Agent, who is subordinate to the Governor-General's agent, residing at Indore. These groups or agencies are respectively—

Indore.	Gwalior.
Bhíl or Bhopawar.	Goona.
Deputy Bhíl.	Bundelkhand.
Western Málwa.	Baghelkhand.
Bhopál.	

General Features.—The Central India Agency occupies the greater part of the triangular plateau that lies to the south-west of the Jumna, and is bounded on the south and south-east by the valleys of the Nerbudda and the Són. The remainder is divided between Rájputána on the west and north-west, the North-West Provinces on the north-east, and the Central Provinces on the south-east; and the districts of the two latter meet across the plateau, separating Baghelkhand and Bundelkhand on the east from the states of the remaining agencies on the west. On the south and east the Central India states stretch across the Nerbudda and Són valleys to the Sátpura range and the hills of Chutia Nágpur.

The surface of the table-land is undulating or hilly, highest on its southern margin, so that the whole of the drainage flows northwards to the Jumna and Ganges. Its elevation varies from 600 to 2000 feet above the sea.

The north-western and the eastern parts, viz. Gwalior, Baghelkhand, and part of Bundelkhand, consist of thick bedded sandstones and other stratified rocks, the edges of which form long escarpments, with an average north-east and south-west direction. Between them, in Bundelkhand, is a wide tract of crystalline rocks dotted with low hummocky hills; and all the south-western part of the plateau is formed of level sheets of basaltic rock, the higher parts of which have been cut into terraced hills by the action of the streams that drain it.

The climate is drier than that of the Gangetic plain, but less so than that of Rájputána. The winter is cool and dry; in the spring the plateau is swept by hot west winds very dry and healthy; and in the rainy season the heat and damp are by no means so oppressive as on the plains of the North-West Provinces or Bengal. Except in the broken and hilly parts, the surface is generally cultivated, the soil of Málwa being especially rich and productive. The eastern and southern parts of the table-land have a rainfall of between 40 and 50 inches in the year, and the hills of South Rewah a still higher amount.

Geographical Position and Area.—The total area of these states is 75,079 square miles, about 13,000 miles less than the island of Great Britain. They lie between 21° 22′ and 26° 53′ N. lat. and between 74° and 82° 46′ E. long., about one-fourth only being south of the Tropic of Cancer or within the torrid zone. Their greatest extension from north-north-east to south-south-west is about 410 miles, and from west to east 520 miles.

Hills and Rivers.—The hills of Central India, like those of Peninsular India generally, are only such more elevated portions of a once more uniform surface as have been left during ages of wasting by the action of the atmosphere and the streams. In Gwalior, Bundelkhand, and Baghelkhand, and bordering the straight valleys of the Nerbudda and the Són, the denuded edges of thick beds of sandstone, limestone, or basaltic rock form escarpments, very steep on one face while the other slopes away gently from the summit. Such are the Vindhya escarpment, which runs for nearly 600 miles parallel to the Nerbudda, bounding its valley on the north; and the Kaimúr escarpment which, farther east, runs for 120 miles to the north of the Són river. The highest summits of the Vindhya are about 2500 feet above the sea, and 1700 feet above the Nerbudda valley at their base. The terraced basaltic hills of Málwa have been already noticed; those of the Sátpura range,

FIG. 14.—THE MARBLE ROCKS, ON THE NERBUDDA.

which form the boundary of the Central Indian territory for about 100 miles to the south of the Nerbudda, are of the same character. This part of the Sátpuras is a belt of hilly country 40 or 50 miles in breadth, the summits averaging 2000 feet above the sea, while many peaks rise to above 3000 feet, and some small table-lands, as Turan Mal, are as high as 4000 feet; this last being 5434 feet at its highest point.

The largest rivers are the Nerbudda, the Són, and the

Chambal; but all have but a part of their course in Central Indian territory. The main stream of the Chambal only skirts its north-west border, and this river has already been noticed under Rájputána (p. 103).

The Nerbudda (Narmada), to Hindu sentiment hardly less sacred than the Ganges, and affording some of the most beautiful river scenery of any Indian river, rises at Amarkantak (3493 feet) in South Rewah, close to the head feeders of the Són and of a large tributary of the Mahánadi (of Orissa). Flowing westwards, and descending by several magnificent falls, after a few miles it enters the Central Provinces, and passing Jubbulpore and traversing a narrow gorge in white marble rock (Fig. 14), it makes its exit on a plain nearly 200 miles long, averaging 20 in width, and elevated more than 1000 feet above the sea. Leaving this below Harda, it enters a wild rocky gorge in the Dhár forest, in which it falls more than 250 feet, and at Barwai, where it re-enters Central Indian territory, emerges on the long narrow plain of Mandlesir, which it traverses for 80 or 90 miles. Finally, plunging into the narrow gorge of Hiran Phal, 70 miles in length, it descends to the plains of Guzerat, where its precipitous course terminates in the great whirlpool of Makrai. From this point to the Gulf of Cambay it is navigable to country boats, but to sea-going vessels only below Broach, distant 30 miles from the sea. The Nerbudda has a total course of 800 miles, and is the largest river that enters the sea through the west coast of the peninsula.

The Són also rises at Amarkantak, flows north and then eastwards for 160 miles through Rewah, along the foot of the Kaimúr range, receiving some considerable tributaries from the hills to the south, but none from the north. It then crosses the Mirzapur district of the North-West Provinces and enters Behar, being joined by the Mohan and Pangan in the former and by the Koel in the latter, all large streams from the hills of Chutia Nágpur. Lastly, emerging from the hills at Dehri, its channel opens out on the plain of South Behar, and it falls into the Ganges above Dinapore.

Neither the Són nor the Nerbudda receives any of the

drainage of the Central Indian plateau. This is all carried off northward to the Jumna and Ganges by the Káli Sindh, the Parbati, and other large tributaries of the Chambal, by the Sindh, the Betwa from Bhopál, the Dhasán a tributary of the Betwa, and the Ken from Bundelkhand, and by the Tons from Baghelkhand. The Tons and some minor rivers farther eastward form magnificent falls of 300 and 400 feet vertical drop, where they cross one of the escarpments in descending from the plateau to the Gangetic plain.

Native States.—The largest and most important of the eighty-two states of Central India are: Indore in the south-west, on the highest part of the table-land; Gwalior in the north-west; Bhopál in the south, and east of Indore; and Rewah, a very hilly state in Baghelkhand, the most eastern portion of the territory. The areas and population of these states are:—

Agency.	State.	Area. Sq. m.	Population.
Gwalior	Gwalior	29,067	3,115,857
Indore	Indore	8,402	1,055,217
Bhopál	Bhopal	6,874	954,901
Baghelkhand	Rewah	10,000 ?	1,305,124

The state of Panna in Bundelkhand, in which there are diamond mines, has an area of 2500 square miles, and all others are less than 2000.

Towns.—The most important place in Central India is Gwalior, the capital of the state so named, with a very strong hill fortress two miles in length, which was the state prison of the Mogul emperors. The present town Lashkar (an army) (pop. 88,000), grew up on the site of the camp of the Maráthá leader Sindia, who took possession of the territory, and whose descendants have since ruled the state. Indore (75,500), Holkar's capital, the residence of the governor-general's agent, on the bank of the Katki river, nearly 2000 feet above the sea. Mhow, at the same altitude, the chief military cantonment in Central India, 13 miles from Indore. Neemuch, another important military station, on the railway about midway between Mhow and Nusseerabad, the chief cantonment of Rájputána. Ujjain

(33,000), in Gwalior, the ancient capital of the province of Málwa, a city of great antiquity and regarded as sacred by the Hindus. In the neighbourhood of Bhopál (55,000) are the Bhílsa and Sánchi topes, Buddhist *stupas* (great dome-shaped masses of masonry erected over relics), which date from the third century B.C. to the first century A.D., and include some of the earliest stone structures known in India.

Population.—In round figures, the population of the Central Indian States is 9¼ millions, of which half a million are Muhammadans and 50,000 Jains. This gives a general average of 123 to the square mile. The Hindu population includes nearly 1 million of Brahmans, over 1 million of the low-caste Chamárs (hide and leather workers), one-third of a million of Gujárs (herdsmen), and a quarter of a million each of Ahírs (herdsmen), Baniyas (trading caste), and Télis (oilmen caste). Other castes are less numerous. Of the aboriginal Gonds there are 413,000, chiefly in the hilly south-eastern states; of the aboriginal Bhíls 217,000, restricted to the south-west corner of the province; and there are 187,000 Kóls, all in the Panna state. Excepting among these aboriginals, the general language of the province is Hindi.

Productions.—There are extensive coalfields in Rewah, as yet but little worked, but they are now being opened out by railways. The state of Panna contains the only diamond mines now worked in Northern India. Most of the territory is well cultivated, producing wheat, rice, and the other usual grains and pulses, also sugar, cotton, and tobacco, and in Indore and the neighbouring little states in the south-west, opium is extensively produced, and is known as Málwa opium. The manufactures are unimportant.

Railways.—The Jubbulpore branch of the East India Railway, which forms part of the present mail route between Calcutta and Bombay, passes across Central India through Soháwal, Sutna, and Myhere. The Sindia State Railway runs from Agra to Gwalior, and is continued to Jhánsi, where it meets the railway from Cawnpore. This line runs on from Jhánsi past Bhílsa to Bhopál, and is continued by the Bhopál State Railway from Bhopál through Hoshangábád to Itarsi on the Great Indian Peninsular Railway. Most of the line from Cawnpore to Bhopál is carried through the territory of the North-West Provinces. A branch leads to Saugor in the Central Provinces.

CENTRAL PROVINCES

Area, 113,279 square miles. Population, 11,548,511

Name and Government.—In 1853, on the death of the ruler of Nágpur, without heirs, that kingdom lapsed to the British Government as the paramount power, and in 1861 it was united with the Saugor and Nerbudda territories on its northern border, and constituted a Chief Commissionership under the name of the Central Provinces. Thus augmented, it nearly coincides with the old states of Gondwána, still so marked on our maps. The name Nágpur (snake city), which was also that of the former state now incorporated in the Central Provinces, is derived from the snake-worship once so prevalent in India, and many traces of which still remain, on the one hand in the frequent appearance of the hooded cobra in Buddhist and Brahmanical sculptures, and on the other in the respect shown to this deadly snake by many of the lower classes of natives. Some of the ruling families of the petty states of Chutia Nágpur are of the *Nágbansi* or "snake-descended" family.

General Features.—Up to the middle of the present century these provinces were the *terra incognita* of India, and in great part a blank on the map. A wild and picturesque region of hill and forest, they have been from time immemorial the special home and refuge of the aboriginal tribes who have eluded the civilising and proselytising influence of the Aryan invaders; and protected by the ramparts and fastnesses furnished by nature, one race, the Gonds, succeeded in organising native governments that, for at least two centuries, maintained themselves amid the more highly developed communities around them. The ancient name of the country, Gondwána, is derived from this race, who still form a large proportion of the population.

Less elevated than many parts of the Mysore and Deccan table-land, from which the central highlands are separated by the valley plains of the Wardha and the Tapti, the surface rises to a local eminence in the Sátpura hills, from which great rivers radiate off in all directions. The north-western half of the province, even on the river plains, is scarcely anywhere less than 1000 feet above the sea, and most of it is occupied by the broken and hilly table-land of the Sátpura system, which averages 2000 feet and, as at Pachmarhi and Amarkantak, rises locally to 3500 feet above the sea-level.

In the south and east of the province, another broad tract of rugged hills and table-lands, in places attaining to a height of 3000 feet, occupies the angle between the Godávari river and the Eastern Ghats, and is separated from the table-land of Hyderabad on the west by the plain of the Wardha and Wainganga rivers, and from the Sátpuras and the Chutia Nágpur table-land on the north by the plain of Chhattísgarh, traversed by the Mahánadi. These plains are fertile and well cultivated. The former slopes from north to south, and from 1300 to 400 feet above the sea; the latter from south-west to north-east, declining from 1300 to 800 feet, where the Mahánadi enters and begins to thread its way through the hills of Sambalpur.

To the north of the Sátpuras, the Central Provinces include the high valley plain of the Nerbudda, already noticed at p. 110, lying between that range and the Vindhyan escarpment; also a strip of the Central Indian table-land north of the Vindhya. The former is a very fertile plain of black soil, all of which is now cultivated; the latter is either gently undulating, with occasional low hills, or consists of generally level tracts of arable land alternating with broken rocky ground that supports but a scanty vegetation; the rocks being partly sandstones, partly flat sheets of basaltic lava.

A large proportion, more than two-thirds of the area of these provinces, is uncultivated, and was at one time covered with forest. And although very much of the larger forest growth has been wasted and denuded, the still-existing forests of teak, sál, and other valuable timbers exceed those of any other province of the Indian peninsula. The forests already reserved and protected cover 3500 square miles.

The climate of the Central Provinces is moderate, especially on the Sátpura plateau, where the hot winds of the early summer months are but little felt. The rainy season is cool and pleasant, and the rains are more regular than in most parts of Northern India, averaging from 40 inches on the driest part of the plains to upwards of 70 inches on certain of the higher hill tracts; severe famines are unknown in most parts of the province.

Position and Area.—The Central Provinces are surrounded by the states of Central India on the north-west, by the Chutia Nágpur division of Bengal on the north-east, by Orissa on the east, the Jeypore state and districts of the Madras Presidency on the south-east, by the Nizam's territory (Hyderabad) on the south-west, and by Berar on the west. They lie between 17° 48′ and 24° 26′ N. lat., and between 76° and 85° 5′ E. long. Their greatest extension is 432 miles from north to south and 576 miles from east to west.

Their total area exceeds 113,000 square miles, or barely 8000 square miles less than the whole of the British Isles, and of this, three-fourths are directly administered by the British Government. At least three-fourths are hill country, and the remainder high plains.

Hills and Rivers.—There is no definite mountain range in the Central Provinces, but the northern part of the province is crossed from east to west by the Sátpura hills, and most of the southern and eastern part is occupied by a series of hill groups and table-lands. The Sátpuras form a long table-land from 40 to 70 miles across, averaging 2000 feet above the sea, and 1000 feet above the lower plains, and consisting of flat sheets of basaltic lava. This is bordered on the north by groups of hills, partly of sandstones with coal-bearing rocks in the valleys, and partly of crystalline rocks. The highest of these is the Pachmarhi or Mahádeo hills, from 3500 to 4500 feet high, sloping gradually to the north, and terminating abruptly on the south in magnificent precipices of sandstone (Fig. 15). The basaltic range terminates on the east in the Maikal and Sálétekri hills, which culminate in Amarkantak (3500 feet).

The Sátpuras send down several tributaries to the Nerbudda, the valley of which bounds the range on the north. This great river has already been described at p. 110. They give rise also to the Tapti, which flows westward, through the Gawilgurh hills, and will be noticed

Fig. 15.—Mahadeo or Pachmarhi Hills from the South.

as a Bombay river; and to the Kanhán and Wainganga flowing southwards. From the eastern flank of the Maikal hills several smaller streams flow eastwards to the Mahánadi.

The Kanhán and Wainganga, after leaving the Sátpuras, unite on the plain of Nágpur, across which the Wainganga flows southwards, and after a course of 350 miles joins the Wardha to form the Pranhíta river; and this, after a farther course of 70 miles, falls into the Godávari at Sironcha.

The hills in the south and south-east of the province are partly ancient slaty rocks and quartzites, partly crystalline rocks. They consist of a number of more or less independent groups, interspersed with small plains. The highest, reaching to 3000 feet, are in the south of the province. They are drained by the Indrávati, a large stream which rises in the Eastern Ghats and flows westwards and then southwards to the Godávari below Sironcha; and by the Mahánadi and its tributaries the Bag, the Jonk, and the Tel, which flow northwards, the three former to the plain of Raipur, the last to its junction with the main stream 50 miles below Sambalpur. The Mahánadi receives also several large affluents from the north, the Seonáth from the Maikal hills, the Hestho from the hills of Korba, farther east, and the Mand and Ib from Chutia Nágpur. It winds its way eastwards and then south-eastwards through the hills of Sambalpur and of the tributary Mehals of Cuttack, and issues on its delta a few miles above the town of Cuttack.

Administrative Divisions.—The province is divided into four commissionerships and eighteen districts, the areas and population of which, exclusive of those of the feudatory native states, are as follows:—

Divisions.	Districts.	Area. Sq. m.	Population.
Nerbudda	Hoshangábád	4,437	488,787
	Narsinghpur	1,916	365,173
	Betúl	3,905	304,905
	Chhindwára	3,915	372,899
	Nimár	3,340	231,341
Jubbulpore	Jubbulpore	3,918	687,233
	Saugor	4,005	564,950
	Damoh	2,799	312,957
	Seoni	3,247	334,733
	Mandla	4,719	301,760
Nagpur	Nágpur	3,786	697,356
	Bhandára	3,922	683,779
	Chándá	10,785	649,146
	Wardha	2,401	387,221
	Bálaghát	3,146	340,554
Chhattísgarh	Raipur	11,885	1,405,171
	Biláspur	7,798	1,017,327
	Sambalpur	4,521	693,499

The Nerbudda division is in the north-west of the province;

it occupies nearly all the Nerbudda valley south of the river, and the western half of the Sátpura range within the province. Nimár is the most westerly and Narsinghpur the most easterly of the valley districts, while Betúl and Chhindwára divide between them the greater part of the Sátpura plateau. In the Jubbulpore division, the most northerly, Saugor and Damoh are on the table-land north of the valley, Jubbulpore partly on its eastern extremity, partly on the northern plateau. Mandla and Seoni lie immediately to the south, wholly in the hill country of the Sátpuras. The great plain to the south of the Sátpuras, east of the Wardha river, constitutes the Nágpur division, and the Bálaghát district includes also the Sálétekri hills. The great district of Chándá occupies all the southern half of the plain. The Chhattísgarh division is in the east of the province, and includes the great plain of Raipur or Chhattísgarh, and the hill tracts on the north, east, and south.

Native States.—Fifteen feudatory native states are included in the Central Provinces, of which Bastar, which occupies most of the wild hill tract drained by the Indrávati in the south of the province, is by far the largest, but the most sparsely populated. Next to this is Kálahandi or Karond, a table-land farther east, bordering on the Eastern Ghats and drained by the Tel river. Pátna, which adjoins it on the north, ranks third. The rulers of these and most of the smaller states claim to be Rájputs. Those of Raigarh and a few others are Gonds. The following are the areas and populations of the states exceeding 1000 square miles :—

States.	Area. Sq. m.	Population.
Bastar	13,062	196,248
Kálahandi	3,745	224,548
Pátna	2,399	257,959
Bámra	1,988	81,286
Raigarh	1,486	128,943

Towns.—Nágpur (pop. 98,000), the capital of the former Maráthá rulers of the state and the present headquarters of the Local Government, is situated on the great central plain south of the Sátpuras. The European quarter is Sitabaldi, with a small hill-fort. Kamptee (51,000), the chief military station of the province, lies 9 miles to the north-east, on the bank of the Kanhán; Jubbulpore (76,000), the second town of the province, at the junction of the East Indian and Great Peninsular Railways, is at the northern foot of the Sátpuras, 1340 feet above the sea. The "School of Industry," established here for the useful employment of reprieved Thugs, is a great tent and carpet manufactory. The gorge of the Nerbudda, known as the "marble rocks" (see Fig. 14), is only 9 miles west of Jubbulpore. Saugor (45,000), an important cantonment with a fine artificial lake, on the basaltic plateau north of the Nerbudda, 109 miles north-west from Jubbulpore. Raipur (25,000), the chief town of the Chhattísgarh division, on the fertile plain of Chhattísgarh, 180 miles east of Nágpur. It is an important mart for agricultural produce, and is a station on the direct line of railway from Calcutta to Bombay; Chándá, the ancient capital of the Chándá Gond dynasty, in the south of the province, surrounded by a still perfect battlemented wall of cut stone, 5½ miles in circuit. The greater part of the enclosure is now cultivated fields, with fine groves of trees, amid which are detached villages with some old buildings; Burhánpur (30,000), a decayed but once large and flourishing town on the north bank of the Tapti, in the Nimár district. Under Akbar and his successors it was the seat of government of the Deccan provinces, and covered 5½ square miles. The rich tissues of silk, cotton, and gold thread for which it was once famous are still produced to some small extent. The hill-station of the province is Pachmarhi, beautifully situated on the little park-like plateau on the summit of the Mahádeo hills, 3500 feet above the sea, and 2500 feet above the plain of the Nerbudda. It is the summer residence of the chief officials of the Government.

Population.—In 1881 the population of the province amounted in round figures to 11½ millions, an average of 102 to the square mile, which is slightly below that of

Assam. In exclusively British territory there were nearly 10 millions, and an average of 117 to the square mile, while in the hilly state of Bastar the average was as low as 15 to the square mile.

The population is more heterogeneous than that of any other Indian province. The aboriginals, classed as such in the census because not yet absorbed into the general Hindu population, numbered 1¾ million, or nearly as many as in Bengal and Chutia Nágpur. The remainder, with the exception of less than 300,000 Muhammadans, are either Hinduised aboriginals or Hindus of Hindi, Maráthá, Telugu, or Uriya race, who in past times have immigrated from the north, west, south, or east respectively. With unimportant exceptions these immigrations have all taken place within the last three centuries. The Hindi-speaking northern immigrants are the most numerous, numbering about 5 millions. They monopolise the northern districts, and penetrate to the south of the Sátpuras. They include Brahmans, Rájputs, Ahírs (herdsmen), Lodhis, Kúrmis (cultivators), and Chamárs (skinners and leather workers); the last very numerous as agriculturists in Biláspur. The Maráthás are chiefly in Nágpur, and do not exceed half a million; the Uriyas, also about half a million, are restricted to Sambalpur; and the Telingas, who are still fewer, to Chándá. They include Brahmans and Kúmbis, Télis (oil-pressers), Kaláls (distillers), Dhímars (fishermen and bearers), Mális (gardeners), and Dhers (outcastes), with many other castes.

Among the aboriginals, the Gonds are the dominant race and are subdivided into many different castes. Their language is Dravidian, nearly allied to the Tamil and Telugu of Southern India. Akin to these are many minor tribes. But there are also numerous tribes of a very different class, speaking languages of a different type, and represented by the Bhumiyas and Dhángars of the eastern, and the Kurkús, Colies, and Bhíls of the western Sátpuras. These are the Kólárian tribes (Fig. 16), and are considered by Col. Dalton to be related to certain tribes of Assam.

Productions.—Although inferior in agricultural capabilities to the Gangetic plain, the Central Provinces are richly productive. The Wardha valley produces some of the finest cotton in India; the Nerbudda valley in the cold season is a vast spread of wheat and pulse crops, and the Chhattísgarh plain, "the granary of Central India," is equally prolific of rice and wheat. The forests yield valuable

FIG. 16.—KORWALI OR KORÉWAHS (KÓLS).

teak and sál timbers, bamboos, stick-lac for the manufacture of lac-gum and dye, tusseh silk, and tanning materials. There are several coalfields, only two or three of which have as yet been worked; and iron ores are abundant, but at present unutilised except to some small extent by rude native processes.

The principal manufactures are cloths of cotton and tusseh silk, but the production of the former is decreasing.

Railways.—The Central Provinces are crossed by two lines of railway, one to the north and one to the south of the Sátpuras; the former being the present mail route between Calcutta and Bombay, the latter, yet unfinished, that which is destined to become so in the future. The Great Indian Peninsular Railway from Bombay divides at Bhosáwul in the Tapti valley, a few miles beyond the western boundary of the province. The northern branch runs through the gap in the Sátpuras opposite Burhánpur, to the Nerbudda valley, and up the valley to Jubbulpore where it meets the Jubbulpore branch of the East Indian Railway from Allahabad. The southern branch ascends the Púrna valley, crosses to the Wardha valley, and terminates at Nágpur. From Nágpur the Bengal and Nágpur Railway runs eastward through Raipur and Biláspur, and then through the wild hilly country of Chutia Nágpur, to join the East Indian Railway at Ránigan j.

The minor railways and branch lines on the Nerbudda branch are—from the Khandwa station a narrow gauge line to Indore and Ajmere; from Itarsi to Hoshangábád and Bhopál, and a short branch to the Mopáni coal-mines. From the Kutni station of the Allahabad and Jubbulpore Railway, one line, still unfinished, runs westwards to Saugor, and another to the south-east to the Umária coalfield (in Rewah), and on to join the Bengal and Nágpur Railway at Bilâspur. From the Bhosáwul and Nágpur Railway a branch runs south to the Warora coalfield, and a short branch to Amraoti.

Bombay

Area, 197,817 square miles. Population, 23,395,663

Name and Government.—The province or presidency of Bombay is so named from the city which is the permanent seat of its government and also its principal port. The name is a corruption of the Maráthá "Mumbai," equivalent to Mahimá (Great Mother), a title of the goddess Devi. The head of the Government is styled the Governor, who is assisted by a council, and the army is under a commander-in-chief, distinct from that of Bengal and the other Northern Provinces. Bombay has also a legislative council and a high court of judicature.

General Features.—The territory under the Bombay Government is a long narrow strip of Western India, including the lower valley of the Indus, and extending down the sea-coast from Cape Monze to about midway in the peninsula. Its surface features and climate are very varied. The province of Sind at its north-western extremity consists of the plain of the lower Indus and its delta, the soil of which is naturally fertile, but the climate is so arid and the rainfall so precarious that its cultivation depends entirely on irrigation from the river. To the east of Sind follow the two great peninsulas of Cutch and Kattywar, consisting of plains surrounding groups and ridges of low hills, and separated from each other by the Gulf of Cutch. These are less dry than Sind, and Kattywar less so than Cutch. Cutch is almost an island, being nearly cut off from the mainland by the Rann, an extensive salt marsh nearly dry during a great part of the year. The marginal portion of the mainland is also included in the province, and is a plain stretching away on the north to the desert tract of Rájputána, and on the east extending up to the foot of the Málwa ghats. On the east the peninsula of Kattywar is bounded by the Gulf of Cambay, into which are discharged the Sábarmati and Mahi from the north, and the Nerbudda and Tapti from the east. The remainder of the province consists of the strip of rugged and hilly but not very elevated country between the west coast of the Indian peninsula and the ghats, called the Konkan and North Kanara, and all the western portion of the Deccan table-land above them; also the high plain of the Tapti lying between the western Sátpuras or Rájpipla hills, and the Indhyádri, Sátmála, or Ajanta range which bounds the Deccan plateau on the north. The Konkan below the ghats and the Deccan above them are alike in the character of their rock structure, both consisting entirely of flat or nearly flat sheets of basaltic lava, which have been worn in the course of ages into flat-topped hills with terraced sides, such as are shown in the accompanying figure of the Bore Ghat (Fig. 17); but in point of climate they are sharply contrasted. The country below the ghats is damp and warm and has a very heavy rainfall, and wherever the forest has not been destroyed the vegetation is rich and tropical; above the ghats, beyond 20 or 30 miles from their crest, the climate is very dry during eight months of the year, and even the monsoon rainfall is light; consequently the surface is nearly treeless, and uncultivated ground is covered with sheets of coarse grass, green only in the rains, brown and withered in the cold season, and when burnt in the spring it presents a very desolate aspect, in the charred surface and naturally black soil unrelieved by the black volcanic rocks.

FIG. 17.—THE BORE GHAT.

Position and Area.—The northernmost point of Sind is in lat. 28° 45′, and the southernmost part of North Kanara in lat. 13° 53′. Cape Monze at the extreme western limit of the former province is in E. long. 66° 40′, and the eastern limit of the Bombay Deccan in E. long. 76° 30′. The greatest extension of the presidency is in a north-north-west and south-south-east direction, amounting to 1026 miles. In a direction transverse to this it nowhere exceeds 300 miles. It covers an area of nearly 198,000 square miles or nearly $1\frac{2}{3}$ times as much as the whole of the British Isles. Of this, rather more than 124,000 square miles are British territory, and the remainder native states, feudatory to the Government of Bombay. These do not include the state of Baroda, which, though surrounded by Bombay territory, is feudatory to the Government of India, and occupies 8570 square miles.

On the north-west the presidency is conterminous with Balúchistán, on the north and north-east with the Punjab and Rájputána, on the east with the Central India states, the Central Provinces, Berar, and Hyderabad; and on the south with Mysore, and below the ghats with the Madras district of South Kanara. Most of the western side is sea-coast.

Hills and Rivers.—To the west of Sind the Khirthar range commences a little to the south of Sehwan and runs northward, forming the boundary of the province and Balúchistán. Entering Balúchistán, it continues to the Bolan Pass, where it is crossed by the Mari and Bhúgti hills running eastward to the Sulemán range. This range has already been noticed under Balúchistán.

In Cutch and Kattywar are some low isolated ridges and groups of hills, the highest of which is Girnar hill, in the south of Kattywar, crowned with Jain temples, and rising to 3666 feet.

On the north-east the Meywar and Málwa Ghats already noticed at p. 102, divide Bombay from Rájputána and Central India to the north of the Nerbudda. To the south of that river the Rájpipla hills, running east and west, form the western extremity of the Sátpura range. Parallel to these but farther eastward and to the south of the Tapti, runs the lower range of the Indhyádri, also called the Ajanta range, after the famous cave temples excavated in their solid rock (see Fig. 5, p. 39). This range divides the upper plain of the Tapti and Púrna (from 700 to 800 feet above the sea) from the higher plateau of the Deccan, drained by the Godávari, and Khandesh from Hyderabad. And beyond the western extremity of the Indhyádri, the Sahyádri range rises to the south of the Tapti and runs first south-west and then south, parallel with the coast, forming the western margin of the Deccan table-land. It is better known as the Western Ghats. It presents a steep declivity to the west, with some summits rising to between 4000 and 5000 feet, but the passes do not much exceed 2000 feet. On the east the general fall is small, but several flat-topped spurs run off into the table-land separating the principal river valleys.

These hills were the home and fastnesses of the petty chiefs who formed the following of Sivâji, the founder of the Maráthá power.

The principal rivers of Bombay are the Indus, the Nerbudda, and the Tapti, all of which have only the final part of their course within the province. The Mahi and Sábarmati are smaller streams which have their head waters in Rájputána, and bring down the drainage of the Meywar and Málwa Ghats. The great rivers of the Deccan plateau are the Godávari, Sina, Bhíma, Kistna, and Tungabhadra.

The Indus has already been described as a river of Kashmír and the Punjab; it enters Upper Sind in a broad, somewhat shifting channel, several miles across when in flood; but opposite Sukkur it is confined by rocks that contract the stream to a few hundred yards. At this point it is now crossed by a large railway bridge on the cantilever principle. A few miles above, at Rohri, it gives off the Nára, the first effluent of its delta, which serves to irrigate Eastern Sind. The Indus flows south-west, then south-east, and then again south-west, passing successively Sehwan, Hyderabad, and Tatta, and after a course of 580 miles from the Punjab frontier, falls into the Arabian Sea. The Nára follows a similar course nearly parallel with the main river, and discharges into the Rann of Cutch. Notwithstanding its great size, the Indus is not navigable to sea-going ships, but country boats can navigate it for about 800 miles from the sea to its exit from the Salt Range.

The Nerbudda has already been noticed as a river of Central India. It can be navigated by small sea-going craft up to Broach, 30 miles from the sea. The Tapti rises in the Sátpura range to the south-east of Betúl in the Central Provinces, traverses the table-land for a few miles, and then plunges into a deep gorge, which gradually opens as it flows to the south-west; but it continues between hills of considerable height and in a narrow valley to Burhánpur; during a part of this course it forms the boundary between the Central Provinces and Berar. Still flowing to south-west it emerges on the high alluvial plain of Khandesh, and 20 miles lower down unites with its great tributary the Púrna, from the plain of Berar. It then turns westward, traversing the whole length of Khandesh. Lastly, descending through the Dangs forest for 60 miles, between the Sahyádri and the Rájpipla hills, it reaches the plain of Guzerat, becomes a tidal stream for the last 32 miles of its course, and passing Surat falls into the Gulf of Cambay. Its total course is 460 miles.

The three largest of the Deccan rivers, the Godávari, the Kistna, and the Tungabhadra have only their head feeders in the Bombay Presidency, and will be noticed more at length under Hyderabad. But the Sina and Bhíma are more truly rivers of the Bombay Deccan. The Sina rises in low hills north of Ahmednagar, passes that city and runs south-east through a hilly country, forming the boundary of the Bombay Presidency and Hyderabad. Near Sholapur it enters on the plain of the Bhíma and shortly afterwards unites with that river. Its course lies through the driest part of the Deccan. The Bhíma is a much larger stream. It receives the drainage of 100 miles of the ghats to the west of Poona, and flows to the south-east through hills till it enters on the dry plain of Pandharpur, which it traverses to its junction with the Sina; and afterwards, flowing eastward, it enters Hyderabad territory. After a further course of about 60 miles it turns to the south and falls into the Kistna.

Administrative Divisions.—The Bombay Presidency, exclusive of Bombay city and island, is subdivided into four commissionerships and 23 districts. These are as follow:

Divisions.	Districts.	Area. Sq. m.	Population.
Sind	Kurrachee	14,115	478,688
	Hyderabad	9,030	754,624
	Shikárpur	10,001	852,986
	Thar and Párkar	12,729	203,344
	Upper Sind Frontier	2,139	124,181
Northern	Ahmedabad	3,821	856,324
	Kaira	1,609	804,800
	Panch Máháls	1,613	255,479
	Broach	1,453	326,930
	Surat	1,662	614,198
	Tanna	4,243	908,548
	Colába	1,496	381,649

Divisions.	Districts.	Area. Sq. m.	Population.
Central	Khandesh	9,944	1,237,231
	Násik	5,940	781,206
	Ahmednagar	6,666	751,228
	Poona	5,348	900,621
	Sholapur	4,521	582,487
	Satara	4,988	1,062,350
Southern	Belgaum	4,657	864,014
	Dharwar	4,535	882,907
	Kaládghi	5,757	638,493
	Kanara	3,911	421,840
	Ratnagiri	3,922	997,090

Sind occupies the delta and valley plain of the lower Indus and the adjacent marginal portion of the desert tract. The Upper Sind Frontier district is a small strip west of the Indus lying under the Bhúgti hills. Shikárpur is the greater part of the plain between the Indus and the Khirthar hills (the rest of which belongs to Balúchistán), and a smaller tract on the left bank of the river adjoining the Punjab. Kurrachee district includes all the western and southern portion of the deltaic tract, and Hyderabad a broad stretch of plain to the east of the river. Thar and Párkar are the arid tract farther east and along the Rann of Cutch.

The northern division comprehends the former state of Guzerat and the country below the ghats (the Konkan) as far south as Mahableshwar. Ahmedabad district is situated north-west of the Gulf of Cambay, Kaira north; the Panch Máháls lie inland to the north-east, and Broach, Surat, Tanna, and Colába follow each other in succession southwards.

The central division lies inland above the ghats. Khandesh is on the high plain of the Tapti. Násik adjoins it on the south, on the higher level of the Deccan plateau. Then follow Poona and Ahmednagar, the former on the west adjoining the ghats, the latter on the east, bounded by the Godávari and the Sina; and Satara and Sholapur lie still farther south.

The southern division includes the country both above and below the ghats; Ratnagiri and Kanara, separated by the Portuguese territory of Goa, in the lower tract; Belgaum and Dharwar on the plateau adjacent to the ghats, and Kaládghi farther east between the Kistna and Bhíma rivers.

Native States.—The native states and chiefships feudatory to the Bombay Government are very numerous; the peninsula of Kattywar alone being divided between 186 such states, and the hilly tracts drained by the Mahi and Sábarmati between 58. Most of the ruling families of these northern states are Rájputs; those of the southern states Maráthás, and those of the Dang forest at the northern end of the ghats, south of the Tapti, of aboriginal descent. The largest states are Khairpur in Upper Sind, Cutch, Pálanpur in Guzerat, Nawanagar and Bhaunagar in Kattywar, and Kolhápur in the Deccan. The areas and population of these are as follow:—

States.	Area. Sq. m.	Population.
Khairpur	6100	129,153
Cutch	6500	512,084
Pálanpur	8000	576,478
Joonagarh	3800	...
Nawanagar	3395	...
Bhaunagar	2784	...
Kolhápur	2816	800,189

The state of Baroda, whose ruler, termed the Gaekwar, is a Maráthá, is feudatory to the Supreme Government of India. His territory, occupying 8570 square miles, with a population in 1881 of 2,185,005, is in detached portions at the north-east corner of the Gulf of Cambay, and east of Surat.

Bombay City.—Bombay, the seat of the Provincial Government, and which came into British possession as the dowry of Catherine of Braganza, the queen of Charles II, is situated at the extremity of a string of islands, now so connected by artificial causeways and the silting up of the intermediate channels as virtually to form a peninsula, which encloses between it and the mainland the most capacious and accessible harbour in India. This great advantage, and also that of its nearness to Europe, were long counterbalanced by its inaccessibility on the land side; by the absence of river communication, and the obstacle to land traffic presented by the Ghat range. Now that the ghats have been surmounted by two railways, and a third opens up communication with Guzerat and North-Western India, the produce of all Central and Western India is readily poured into Bombay, while the Suez Canal has opened up direct communication with Europe. Thus, from being second to Calcutta, it has now risen to the first place as a great commercial port, and it is the great cotton mart of the East. It is the seat of a university, of the chief magnetic observatory in India, and of three scientific societies. The old fort, now dismantled, is the mercantile centre, and noble public buildings have been erected on the site of the old fortifications. The native city, farther north, is very extensive and extremely picturesque. Large docks have been constructed on the harbour face, and numerous cotton mills have been established on its northern outskirts. Malabar hill, on the sea-face of the island, is covered with the suburban residences of the officials and wealthy residents. Altogether the city and its suburbs cover 22 square miles, and the population, in 1881, exceeded three-quarters of a million (773,000). On the island of Elephanta, in the harbour, are the famous Brahmanical cave temples, excavated about the eighth century.

Other Towns and Places of Importance.—Besides Bombay, three cities in the Presidency, and Baroda (102,000) the capital of that state, have each more than 100,000 inhabitants. These are Poona (130,000), Ahmedabad (128,000), and Surat (110,000). Poona, the former capital of the Peishwa (the Maráthá ruler) and the present summer residence of the Bombay Government, is above the ghats (1850 feet), 119 miles south-east from Bombay. It is reached by the railway up the Bore Ghat (see Fig. 17), hard by which are the famous Kárla caves, and many other rock temples of the Buddhist period. Ahmedabad, the capital of the former Muhammadan state of Guzerat, founded by Ahmed Shah, the ruler of that state in the fifteenth century, is still a splendid city. In the sixteenth and seventeenth centuries it is stated to have had nearly a million of inhabitants. Surat, the chief port of India in the time of the great Mogul emperors, is situated on the Tapti estuary, fourteen miles from the sea. The first English factory in India was established here in 1612.

Next in importance to these are, in Sind, Kurrachee (Karáchi) (73,500), the seaport of the Indus valley, situated near the south-west corner of the delta, between it and Cape Monze. It is the terminus of the Indus valley railway, which brings down the produce of the Punjab. Hyderabad (48,000), the former capital of the Amírs of Sind, on a low eminence three miles from the Indus. The tombs of the Amírs are conspicuous to the north of the city. Shikárpur (42,000) the chief town of Upper Sind and the centre of the trade between Sind and the countries beyond the Bolan Pass. Jacobabad (11,000), founded by General John Jacob, on the border of the Kach Gandava desert, 26 miles from Shikárpur, an important military frontier station. In Kattywar and Guzerat, Bhaunagar (48,000) and Nawanagar (40,000) two ports on the Gulf of Cambay. Deesa (Dísa) (6000) the chief military station of the northern districts. Broach (37,000), a port for coasting craft on the Nerbudda estuary, 30 miles from the sea; still an important commercial town, but inferior to Surat.

On the west coast south of Bombay, Kárwar (13,500) with the best harbour on the west coast next to Bombay. In the Deccan, Násik (27,000) on the Godávari, an ancient Hindu city, with numerous temples, and with richly decorated Buddhist caves of the first century in the neighbourhood; the old Muhammadan capitals of Ahmednagar (37,500) on the Sina, and Bijápur (13,000) in the Kaládghi district, with splendid architectural remains. Belgaum (33,000) the chief military station of the southern division, 20 miles from the crest of the ghats, and 2500 feet above the sea; and Hubli (37,000) in Dharwar, the centre of the cotton trade of the southern districts.

The chief hill station of the Presidency is Mahableshwar (4540 feet), on one of the highest summits of the Ghat range, in the Satara district. It is but little frequented in the rainy season, owing to the very heavy rainfall (260 inches). The little hill station of Matheran, on a detached hill near the foot of the Bore Ghat, is readily accessible from Bombay, and although low (2200 feet), is a favourite temporary resort from the capital.

Population and Languages.—The census of 1881 gave the total population of the Presidency as 23,395,663, in round figures, 23½ millions, being an average of 118 to the square mile. In the Thar and Párkar district, and in the Dangs forest, it is as low as 16, and in the Surat district as high as 360 to the square mile. About 16¼ millions are in British territory.

Three-fourths of the population are Hindus. Muhammadans contribute rather more than 18 per cent and Jains 1⅓. Parsis, though far more numerous than in any other Indian province, amount to only 0·4 per cent; and of aboriginals, not yet absorbed into the low-caste Hindu population, there are somewhat under a million. Muhammadans are most numerous in Sind, Rájputs in Kattywar, and in the Deccan the mass of the population are Maráthás, who are regarded by the Brahmans as Sudras, but claim to be Kshetryas. The numerous caste of Maráthá-Brahmans (Fig. 18), a highly intellectual race, are of different descent. The cultivators of Guzerat are mostly Kulambis and Ahírs, those of the Deccan Kúnbis.

The aboriginal tribes are most numerous in the hills north and east of Guzerat, the Dangs, the Ghats and the hills that branch off from them. They are termed Bhíls in the north-eastern hills and Khandesh, and Colis (whence the common term "cooly" for an unskilled labourer) in Guzerat and the south. They appear to be nearly akin to each other and to be both of Kolárian race, but they retain but little if any of their original language. The Colis have acquired more civilisation than the Bhíls, and in most parts of the Presidency they are more or less absorbed into the low-caste Hindu population.

The chief languages of the Bombay Presidency are Sindhi, Guzeráti (which besides being the language of the province is generally used in commercial transactions), Maráthi in the northern Deccan and most of the Konkan, Konkani in the North Kanara district, and Canarese in the southern districts of the Deccan. All but the last are Prakritic (Sanskritic) languages; Canarese alone being Dravidian and nearly allied to the languages of Southern India.

Productions.—Nearly half of the Presidency being formed of sheets of basaltic lava, and much of the remainder covered with alluvial clays and sands, it yields but few useful minerals other than building stones. Agates are common in certain of the volcanic rocks and are worked at

Fig. 18.—Maráthá Pandits (Brahmans).

Cambay. Salt is manufactured on the coast by evaporating sea-water.

Wheat is largely grown in Khandesh and Guzerat, and other grains and pulses as elsewhere, but the chief crop for export is cotton. Guzerat, Khandesh, and the Deccan produce some of the best kinds of cotton in India, and the exports are very large of both the raw and manufactured material. Spinning mills and calico factories are numerous in Bombay, Broach, and Surat, and hand-weaving is carried on throughout the Presidency, and especially at Ahmedabad, Ahmednagar, Malegaon, Násik, Poona, and Dharwar. Rich silk fabrics and those interwoven with silver and gold are also produced in the old native capitals and at Bombay; and paper is made at Ahmedabad, Baroda, Surat, Násik, Bombay, and Kolhápur. Ahmednagar and Cutch are famous for their silver work, and Sind for embroidery and pottery. High-class pottery is also produced at Bombay.

Railways.—Two main lines of railway start from Bombay, viz. the Bombay and Baroda Railway running northwards along the coast, through Surat and Broach to Baroda and Ahmedabad, and the Great Indian Peninsular Railway eastwards. From Ahmedabad the Rájputána State Railway carries on the communication to Ajmere, Delhi, Agra, and the Punjab and North-West Provinces, and the Bombay line runs westwards to Kattywar, where it meets the Bhaunagar Gondal Railway which leads to Bhaunagar on the Gulf of Cambay and to Dhoraji. There are also minor branches.

The Great Indian Peninsular Railway divides at Callian below the ghats; one branch ascends the Thal Ghat to Násik and Bhosáwal, beyond which it traverses Berar to Nágpur and the Central Provinces to Jubbulpore, where it meets the East India Railway; the other ascends the Bore Ghat (see Fig. 17) to Poona, and then proceeds eastward to Sholapur and southward to Raichur in Hyderabad where it meets the Madras Railway. A cross line, the Dhond and Manmad Railway, connects these two branches above the ghats, passing through Ahmednagar.

From Poona and Sholapur two lines belonging to the South Maráthá Railway system communicate with the southern districts of the Presidency. The west Deccan section from Poona runs south through Satara, Kolhápur, and Belgaum, the east Deccan section from near Sholapur south through Bijápur, and both terminate at their junction with the line that runs westward from Bellary through Hubli and Dharwar and down the ghats to Marmugao on the sea-coast, where a harbour has been constructed not far from Goa. In Sind, the Indus Valley State Railway, starting from Kurrachee, runs north-east to Kotri on the Indus opposite to Hyderabad, with which there is communication by a steam ferry; it then follows up the right bank of the Indus to Sukkur, where a cantilever bridge carries it across the river to Rohri on the left bank, and from this place it runs north-east parallel with the river to Buháwalpur, and on to Mooltan and Lahore.

From Ruk between Rohri and Shikárpur, the Sind-Pishín or Kandahar State Railway branches off, running through Shikárpur, Jacobabad, and Sibi to Quetta and Pishín.

BERAR

Area, 17,711 square miles. Population, 2,672,673

Name and Government.—Berar (Warar) is so named from the Wardha river which forms its eastern boundary. It was formerly a part of Hyderabad, and became a British Province in 1853. It is administered by a commissioner who is subordinate to the Resident at Hyderabad, the surplus revenue being paid to the Nizam.

General Features.—The province consists of the high plain of the Púrna river, which is a westward extension of the plain of Khandesh, also of the Gawilgurh hills, a high group of the Sátpura range on the north, the Indhyádri or Ajanta range on the south, and the upper valleys of the Penganga or Pranhíta and its tributaries beyond. The greater part of its southern boundary is formed by the Penganga and its eastern boundary by the Wardha. Thus it consists of a plain from 800 to 1200 feet above the sea, and as much or more below the hills to the north and south. The Gawilgurh hills consists of valuable forests, and the plain of the Púrna is covered with black "cotton soil" all cultivated. The climate is very similar to that of Khandesh and the Bombay Deccan, and drier than that of the Central Provinces.

Position and Area.—The total area of Berar is 17,711 square miles or rather more than half that of Ireland, of which total the plain country occupies somewhat less than half. It lies between 21° 48′ and 19° 32′ N. lat., and between 76° and 79° 12′ E. long., and extends about 200 miles from west-north-west to east-south-east, and 160 miles in a transverse direction. It is surrounded by the Central Provinces on the north and east, by Hyderabad on the south, and by the same state and the Khandesh district of Bombay on the west.

Hills and Rivers.—The Gawilgurh hills on the north rise to between 3000 and 4000 feet. The Ajanta range on the south nowhere much exceeds 2000 feet, and has a general direction from west-north-west to east-south-east. Both consist of volcanic rocks like the hills of the Deccan and Hyderabad.

The chief rivers are—the Tapti (already noticed under Bombay), the Púrna, the Penganga, and the Wardha. The Púrna rises in the hills to the north and flows westwards across the Berar plain to the Tapti. The Penganga has its head-waters in the Ajanta range, near Buldana, at the south-western extremity of the province, and flows eastwards in a somewhat tortuous course through hills, receiving the drainage of the southern face of the Ajanta range, till it unites with the Wardha at its south-eastern extremity. The Wardha rises in the Sátpuras near Betúl, in the Central Provinces, and leaving the hills flows to the south-east through a fertile plain to its junction with the Penganga, 190 miles from its source. Its further course is across the plain of Wardha and Chándá, where it unites with the Wainganga and eventually falls into the Godávari.

Administrative Divisions.—The province is subdivided into six districts under deputy-commissioners, as follow :—

Districts.	Area. Sq. m.	Population.
Amráoti	2759	575,328
Akola	2660	592,792
Ellichpur	2623	313,805
Buldána	2804	439,763
Wún	3907	392,102
Básim	2958	358,883

Akola occupies most of the western half and Amráoti the eastern half of the Berar plain ; Ellichpur, a small tract between them to the north of the Púrna, together with the Gawilgurh hills. Buldána includes the western end of the hill tract south of the valley and a small part of the plain itself. Básim to the east of it, the remainder of the

Ajanta hills, and Wún all the south-eastern end of the province. It is a wild tract consisting of small undulating plains interspersed with hills.

Towns.—The two most important towns are Akola (17,500), and Amráoti (23,500), where reside the chief government officials; the latter being also one of the great cotton marts of the province. The other is Khamgaon in the Akola district. Ellichpur (26,700) is an old native capital and a military cantonment. Chikalda, at an elevation of 3777 feet on the Gawilgurh hills, 20 miles from Ellichpur, is the hill sanitarium of the province.

Population.—The population of Berar in round figures is $2\frac{2}{3}$ millions, an average of 151 to the square mile. The most thickly peopled districts are those of the Púrna plain, where the average is about 215 to the square mile. In the jungly district of Wún it does not exceed 100 to the square mile.

Hindus form 91 per cent of the population. The cultivators are chiefly Kúnbis as in the northern Bombay Deccan; a quiet, unwarlike, and fairly industrious race. The language of the province is mainly Maráthi. In the Gawilgurh hills is an aboriginal tribe termed "Cooars" or "Kúrkus," speaking a Kolarian language.

Productions.—As mentioned above, the greater part of the province is covered with volcanic rock, but the eastern part of the Wún district along the Wardha river is a basin of coal-bearing rocks, continuous with that of Warora and Chánda on the left bank of the river. It is the north-western extremity of an enormous stretch of these rocks, which extends down the valleys of the Wardha and the Godávari nearly to the coast, and is worked for coal in the Central Provinces and the Hyderabad state. Carbonate of soda is deposited from the waters of a remarkable lake, having the appearance of a volcanic crater, at Lonar, in the south of the Buldána district.

The chief agricultural produce is cotton, millets, and oil seeds, with some wheat; and there are valuable reserved forests on the Gawilgurh hills.

Railways.—The Púrna valley is traversed by the Nágpur branch of the Great Peninsular Railway from

Bhosawal. It passes Akola and communicates by short branch lines with Amráoti and Khamgaon.

HYDERABAD

Area, 81,807 square miles. Population, 9,845,594

Name and Government.—Hyderabad, known also as the Nizam's territory, is the largest and most important feudatory state in India. The name is that of the capital city, which was called after the son of its founder. The Nizam, its ruler, is a Muhammadan prince, descended from the soldier who was appointed viceroy of the Deccan under Aurungzib, with the title of Nizam-ul-Mulk, and became independent on the break up of the Mogul Empire. The Supreme Government of India is represented at the capital by an official termed the Resident.

General Features.—The Hyderabad state occupies the heart of the peninsula and of the Deccan table-land, with an average elevation of 1250 feet above sea-level, and with a general slope from west to east. The western half consists of plains of black cotton soil, alternating with ranges of the low flat-topped, terraced hills, characteristic of the great basaltic formation of the Deccan; the eastern half chiefly of rolling plains of crystalline rocks, with grouped or isolated hills; often weathering into rounded hummocks and tors of bare rock, which are very numerous close to the capital city. A large field of the coal-bearing rocks runs along the eastern margin of the state, and furnishes a sandy and not very fertile soil, but as far as is known these beds are less rich in coal than those of the same formation in Chutia Nágpur and Bengal.

There is but little forest of any value in the state, and in the western districts trees are rare. Large tracts are uncultivated, and irrigation is obtained only from tanks formed by embanking natural depressions of the surface. The eastern districts, and especially the country around Warangal, the ancient capital of Telingána, are dotted over with such tanks, some of great size, constructed by the Hindu rulers who preceded the Muhammadans. That of

Pakhal in the Khamam district is 30 miles in circumference and probably the largest in India.

The climate of Hyderabad, like that of the Bombay Deccan, is dry and moderate; cool but not cold in the winter months, hot in the spring and early summer, and cool and cloudy but not very wet in the rainy season, when the surface is swept by a strong west wind. The rainfall averages 32 inches in the year, rising to 40 in the neighbourhood of the Godávari, and falling below 30 in the west and south.

Position and Area.—The boundary of the Nizam's territory forms an irregular four-sided figure, the longest sides of which face to the west and south-east. It is demarcated on the north by the Ajanta range and the Penganga river, on the north-east by the Wardha, the Pranhíta, and the Godávari, on the south-east by the Tungabhadra and the Kistna, and on the west partly by the Sina, and for a short distance by the Godávari. It is surrounded on the west and north-west by the Bombay Presidency, on the north by Berar, on the north-east by the Central Provinces, and on the south by the Presidency of Madras. It lies between the parallels of 20° 41′ and 15° 10′ N. lat., and between the meridians of 74° 47′ and 81° 32′ E. long., and extends 420 miles from north to south and about 380 miles from west to east. Its total area is 81,807 square miles, which is slightly greater than that of England and Scotland, without Wales.

Hills and Rivers.—As in other parts of the Indian peninsula, the hills of Hyderabad are merely those portions of the once more uniform surface that have remained above the general level after ages of wasting by the action of the atmosphere and the rivers. In the west the rivers, all of which flow eastwards, have cut their valleys in such a manner as to leave terraced flat-topped spurs of basaltic rock running in the same general direction. The most prominent of these are in the north of the state, viz. the Ajanta range, separating the head waters of the Hyderabad Púrna (a tributary of the Godávari) from the Tapti and the Púrna of Berar; and two ranges which run off from this to the south-east, between the Penganga and Hyderabad

Púrna and between the latter and the Dudna respectively. To the south of the Godávari another ridge separates the valley of that river from the higher plateau drained by the Manjira. In the east of the state are some groups of whale-backed hills of crystalline rocks having no definite prevailing direction.

The chief rivers are the Godávari, with its northern tributaries the Dudna and Púrna, and its great southern tributary the Manjira; and the Kistna, with its tributaries the Bhíma and Tungabhadra. The Godávari rises in the Sahyádri range, north of Násik, and after a course of 90 miles across the Bombay Deccan, runs along the boundary of the state for another 70 miles; then crossing Hyderabad territory in a direction somewhat to the south of east for 245 miles and receiving the united waters of the Dudna and the Púrna, it unites with the Manjira from the south. After a further course of 190 miles eastward, it receives the Pranhíta (already noticed as a river of the Central Provinces). It then turns to the south-east, forming the boundary of the Hyderabad state and the Central Provinces for 150 miles. Lastly, breaking through the eastern ghats in a narrow gorge and entering the Madras Presidency, the stream opens out on its delta at Rajahmundry, and discharges itself into the Bay of Bengal after a total course of 900 miles. Only 200 miles of the upper part of the river is navigable from June to February, and this portion is not accessible from the coast, communication being barred by two rocky barriers, one below Sironcha, and another between Dumagudhem and Bhadráchallam.

The Kistna river rises in the ghats at Mahableshwar, and in the first 320 miles of its course runs first due south between the hills, then south-east, and then eastward across the Bombay Deccan, receiving several large tributaries from the Ghat range. For the next 10 miles it skirts the Hyderabad state, then entering Hyderabad territory, it turns to north-east for 75 miles. Again bending to south-east it receives the Bhíma, and after holding this course for 80 miles to its junction with the Tungabhadra, it changes to east-north-east, flowing for 180 miles along the boundary of the state in a rocky channel between two of the parallel hill ranges that here form the Eastern Ghats. Finally escaping on the plains of Madras and passing Bezváda, it branches out on its delta and falls into the Bay of Bengal immediately to the south of the Godávari. Its total course is 750 miles.

The great tributary of the Kistna, the Tungabhadra, is formed by the junction of two rivers, the Tunga and the Bhadra, which rise on the crest of the Western Ghats of Mysore. It runs north-east across the plateau, forming the boundary first of the Bombay Presidency and Mysore, and then of Hyderabad and Madras, and after a total course of 370 miles from its sources unites with the Kistna below Kurnool. The head feeders of the Kistna and Tungabhadra together carry off the drainage of about 350 miles of the Ghat range, but their subsequent course is across the driest part of the peninsula.

Administrative Divisions.—The Nizam's dominions are subdivided, on the same general plan as the British provinces of India, into divisions and districts, as follow :—

Divisions.	Districts.	Area. Sq. Miles.	Population.
Western	Bidar	4884	793,309
	Nánder	4122	753,035
	Naldurg	3997	538,807
	Yelgandal	7480	961,172
	Indur	3945	562,798
Northern	Medak	1779	293,930
	Sirpur Tandur	5022	214,231
	Aurungabad	6159	729,298
North west	Parbhani	4334	582,379
	Birh	4487	560,960
Eastern	Khamam	9778	675,746
	Nagar Karnul	5573	547,694
	Nalgonda	4131	494,190
	Gulbarga	4011	470,425
	Linsugúr	3371	330,199
Southern	Ráichur	2338	315,109
	Shorapur	2901	287,602
	Atrafa Balda	3438	379,748
	Hyderabad City	3	123,675
	,, Suburbs	45	231,287

Towns and Important Places.—The city of Hyderabad is situated on a stony plain on the right bank of the Moosa, a small tributary of the Kistna, 1660 feet above the sea. Its suburb, Secunderabad, is the largest British cantonment in Southern India, and is on higher ground (1800 feet). The old capital and fort of Golconda, now the Nizam's treasury and also a prison, lie seven miles to the west. Other old capitals still retaining vestiges of their former magnificence are—Warangal, the royal city of the Hindu rajahs of Telingána; Bidar, on the Manjira river, that of the Bahmani kings of the Deccan, and later, that of the Barid Shahi dynasty of the petty Bidar state; it gives its name to the inlaid metal ware there manufactured and known as Bidri ware; Gulbarga (23,000), another capital of the Bahmani princes; Aurungabad (30,000) on the Dudna, that of Nizam Shahi dynasty in the seventeenth century. Ten miles to the north-west is the historic fortress of Deogiri and the city of Daulatabad, and 13 miles off in the same direction the famous sculptured caves of Ellora. Again, 40 miles to the north-east, is the battle-field of Assaye, and hard by, the Buddhist caves and rock temples of Ajanta (see Fig. 5, p. 39), with fresco paintings of the early centuries of the Christian era; Jálna, a military cantonment, is 38 miles east of Aurungabad.

Population.—The population of Hyderabad state, according to the last census, was nearly ten millions, of which about one-tenth were Muhammadans, therefore of the religion of the rulers, and the remainder, with unimportant exceptions, Hindus. The general average is 120 to the square mile. The most thinly populated districts are Sirpur Tandur, and Khamam, both hilly tracts, one in the north-east, the other in the east of the state, bordering on the Godávari. Brahmans contribute about a quarter of a million; among the cultivators the most numerous castes are Kúnbis, numbering $1\frac{2}{3}$ millions. Of aboriginal Dhángars and Colis there are about 700,000.

Three languages are spoken in different parts of the state. Maráthi in the north and west; Canarese in the south-west; and Telugu in the south-east. The two latter are Dravidian.

Productions.—Coal is mined in the south-east of the

state, but at present only on a small scale. The diamond mines, known to fame as those of Golconda, are beyond the border of the Hyderabad state in the Madras Presidency. In the Linsugúr district, in the south-west corner of the state, is a band of auriferous rocks (similar to those of Mysore) which have at one time been extensively worked for gold. Of agricultural produce, cotton and oil seeds are raised for export. The chief manufactures are cotton cloths and the rich gold embroidered fabrics made at the old capitals Aurungabad, Gulbarga, etc. Warangal is noted for fine carpets and rugs, and Hyderabad for mixed fabrics of silk and cotton. The inlaid metal ware of Bidar has been already noticed. Excellent paper is made at Kághazpur (Paper town) near Daulatabad.

Railways.—The state is traversed from the north-west by the Great Peninsular Railway, and from the south by the Madras Railway, which meet at Raichur and form part of the mail line between Bombay and Madras. From Wadi, a station on this line, the Nizam's State Railway runs east to Hyderabad and on to Warangal, Khamam, and Bezváda on the Kistna below the ghats.

Mysore and Coorg

Area—Mysore, 24,723 square miles ; Coorg, 1583 square miles.
Population—Mysore, 4,186,188 ; Coorg, 178,302

Name and Government.—The native state of Mysore is named after a buffalo-headed monster (Mahesh-asura) of Indian mythology. It became a British possession in 1799 on the defeat and death of its Muhammadan ruler Tipu, and was made over to a descendant of its former Hindu rajahs; but in consequence of his proved incapacity, the British administration of the province was resumed in 1831, and continued till 1881, when the present Rajah was invested with the princely office as an act of grace. The Imperial Government is now represented by the Resident of Mysore, who is also commissioner of Coorg.

Coorg (*Kodagu*, crooked) is a little state in the hills of the Western Ghats, bordering on Mysore. It came under

British administration in 1834, and is administered by the government of India, through the Resident of Mysore.

General Features.—Mysore occupies the most southern and also the highest portion of the central plateau of the peninsula, bordered by the Eastern and Western Ghats. It is of triangular form, the two Ghat ranges converging at its southern extremity in the little lofty table-land of the Nilgiri hills. Its surface is gently undulating, between 2000 and 3000 feet above the sea, consisting of crystalline rocks which weather into tors and isolated rocky hills, many of which are crowned with *droogs* or hill-forts, the strongholds of the *poligars* or petty chieftains who maintained their independence in the troublous times of the eighteenth century. Between the drainage basins of the Tungabhadra and the Cauvery are some groups of loftier hills, some summits of which rise to over 6000 feet, and many to 4000 or 5000 feet. The hilly country bordering on the Western Ghats, the *Malnad*, is well watered and covered with evergreen forest and coffee plantations, but the rolling plains to the eastward are much drier and have more than once been devastated by severe famines. Cultivation is carried on by irrigation from tanks, with which the country is thickly dotted, and which are fed from the rivers.

Position and Area.—The Mysore state lies between 11° 37′ and 14° N. lat., and between 74° 42′ and 78° 38′ E. long., and extends 225 miles from north to south and rather more from east to west. It covers an area of 24,723 square miles, or about 5000 square miles less than Scotland. It is surrounded by the Bombay presidency on the north-west, and by the Madras presidency on other sides, excepting for about 70 miles of its south-west frontier, when it is conterminous with the little state of Coorg.

Coorg has an area of only 1583 square miles, and measures 70 miles from north to south, and at its widest 40 miles from west to east.

Hills and Rivers.—The principal ranges of hills are the Eastern and Western Ghats, the crests of which in places form the boundary of Mysore. The highest points of the latter are Tadiandamol peak in Coorg (5729 feet), Subrahmanyah (5583 feet), and Kodachadri (4446 feet), on the borders of Mysore. The former culminate in the Bilgirirangan hills (5500 feet), south-east of Mysore. Higher than any of these are the Bababudan hills in the north-west of the state, separating the head waters of the Tunga, Bhadra, and Varada, all rivers of the Kistna drainage system, from those of the Hemavati, the northernmost feeder of the Cauvery. Two summits of this group rise to 6317 and 6215 feet. In the east of the state three broken ranges run northward, separating the Kistna drainage from that of the Pennér and some smaller streams that run eastward. The highest of these hills are between 4000 and 5000 feet. Besides these, are numerous smaller groups ranging between 3000 and 4500 feet.

All the north of the state is drained by the Tunga-bhadra and its tributaries, the largest of which is the Vedavati or Hagari; and all the south is the basin of the Cauvery river. The course of the former has already been noticed under Hyderabad; that of the latter will be described under Madras. In the east are the sources of the Pennér flowing northward, and those of the Pálár and Púngani, the former flowing eastward, the latter southward into the Carnatic, where it takes the name of the Ponniár. In the north-west, a small river, the Sheravati, which rises to the east of the Ghat range near Nagar, after a course of 50 miles to the north-west, breaks through the Western Ghats and discharges itself on the west coast. In its descent at Gérsapa, it precipitates itself in an unbroken fall of 832 feet, which is described as being one of the most magnificent cataracts on the globe.

Administrative Divisions.—Mysore state is divided into three divisions and eight districts, the extent and population of which are respectively as follow :—

Division.	Districts.	Area. Sq. m.	Population
Nundydroog . . .	Bangalore	2901	669,139
	Kolar	1891	461,129
	Túmkúr	3420	413,183

Divisions.	Districts.	Area. Sq. m.	Population.
Ashtagram	Mysore	2980	902,566
	Hassan	1879	535,806
Nagar	Shimoga	3797	499,728
	Kadur	2984	328,327
	Chitaldroog	4871	376,310

Kolar occupies the eastern corner, and Bangalore and Túmkúr adjoin it on the west. Mysore is the southernmost district, and Hassan, Kadur, and Shimoga succeed each other to the north-west, bordering on the Western Ghats; while Chitaldroog lies centrally in the north of the state.

Towns.—Bangalore (156,000), situated on one of the highest parts of the Mysore plateau (3000 feet), is the chief civil station and a large British cantonment. It has the finest climate of any station in Southern India (excepting those on the Nilgiris). Mysore (60,000), the old native capital, ten miles from which is Seringapatam (12,000), a strong fortress on an island in the Cauvery. It was stormed by the British army under General Harris in 1799, when Tipu was slain in the breach, and the country became a British possession. Mercára, the chief town of Coorg, is on a little plateau 3800 feet above the sea, overlooking the ghats. Its climate is cool and pleasant, except in the rainy season, when for weeks together it is shrouded in cloud.

Population.—In 1881 the population of Mysore was rather over 4 millions, an average of 169 to the square mile. Ten years previously, before the disastrous famine of 1876, it was over 5 millions, the loss of life in Mysore having been proportionally greater than in any other part of India. Nearly 4 millions of the population are classed as Hindus, the Muhammadans scarcely exceeding 200,000, but the former include semi-Hinduised aboriginals and a certain number of Jains. Canarese is the prevailing language of the state.

The people of Coorg are a distinct and independent race of mountaineers, having a peculiar national dress, and for their active loyalty in 1857 they were specially exempted from the disarming Act. They number 178,000.

Productions.—Of late years the chief mineral product of Mysore is gold. The hard granitoid rocks of the plateau are traversed from north-west to south-east by parallel bands of schistose rocks of a somewhat later formation, in which occur quartz-reefs and veins, some of them highly auriferous. These are now being exploited with the aid of European machinery. Most of the sandal-wood of India is yielded by the forests of the dry tract of Mysore, where it is a state monopoly; and most of the Indian coffee is produced either in Mysore, especially in the Baba-budan hills (where it was first introduced from Arabia), in Coorg, or the adjacent tract of the Wynaad in Madras. Rági, a small millet, is the staple food of the people and is also exported. A peculiar kind of printed cloth is manufactured at Bangalore.

Railways.—Bangalore is reached from Madras by a branch of the Madras Railway, and is connected with Mysore by the Mysore State Railway, and with Túmkúr on the north-west by a branch of the same line.

Madras

Area, 149,538 square miles. Population, 34,213,353

Name and Government.—The presidency of Madras or Fort St. George is so named from the chief town (Mandráj-patnam). The etymology of Mandráj is uncertain. The first presidency in India was established here in 1653. Like Bombay, Madras has a governor and council, a legislative council, a high court, and its army is the separate command of a commander-in-chief.

General Features.—The territory of the presidency includes all the peninsula south of Mysore, the coast tract and Ghat ranges as far north as the limits of Bombay, in lat. 13° 53′ on the west, and those of Orissa in lat. 20° 25′ on the east; also a strip of the central plateau lying between Hyderabad and Mysore. The Eastern and Western Ghats converge in the Nilgiri hills, to the south of which the uplands of the interior are interrupted for a space of about 25 miles by the Pálghat gap, where the lower plain, with a maximum elevation of about 800 feet, stretches across from sea to sea. South of this gap the hills rise again to an elevation equal to that of the Nilgiris, and a range of varying height and width continues down the western side of the peninsula nearly to Cape Comorin. The coast plain to the west of these hills is rugged and narrow, with a fringe of alluvial formation enclosing long lagoons or backwaters, which admit of continuous inland navigation for long distances. The eastern coast plain, that of the Carnatic, is of variable width, averaging about 80 miles, and where narrowest, to the north of Madras, 30 miles across. It consists of alluvial flats around the lower course of the rivers that descend from the Eastern Ghats, and nearly continuous along the coast. These portions are highly cultivated, and irrigated from tanks formed by embanking natural depressions on their borders and frequently many miles in extent. The higher ground, covered with a sandy soil, is occasionally cultivated with dry crops, but very much of it is rocky, unculturable, and covered with low scrub. Between the coast plain and the ghats rise several extensive groups of hills, more or less isolated, and varying from 3000 to 5000 feet in height, and the higher parts of the plain are dotted over with tors, such as that represented in Fig. 19, and bold rocky hills, often crowned with hill-forts.

The richest portions of the Carnatic are the great deltas of the Godávari, the Kistna, and the Cauvery, where agriculture is ensured by elaborate systems of irrigation, supplied by canals taken off from the main streams; great dams, termed *annicuts*, being thrown across them at the heads of their deltas.

The Western Ghats, under the heavy rainfall of the westerly monsoon, are clothed with dense tropical forest; the Eastern Ghats and the east face of the Travancore hills are drier and afforested only in parts, and of that portion to the north of Madras, up to the Kistna river, very much is bare and rocky.

The districts on the central plateau are similar to the adjacent portions of Mysore, rolling rocky plains with occasional hills, and being situated in the driest part of the peninsula, trees are rare and agriculture somewhat precarious.

The climate of the west coast is very damp and the temperature high, varying but little throughout the year. That of the east coast is drier; and in the Carnatic the heavy rainfall of the year does not set in till October, when the rains are over in North-Western India. Excepting for about six weeks in December and January, the climate is warm throughout the year, but never so hot as in North-

FIG. 19.—TOR AT MALAVANUR IN THE CARNATIC.

Western India. On the plateau of the interior the climate is very dry and the rainfall light, and this is equally the case on the lower plain of Coimbatore and that of Tinnevelly in the south. To the north of the Godávari the monsoon rainfall is more copious than in the Carnatic, and but little later than in Northern India.

Position and Area.—As may be seen on the map, the Madras province is of very irregular form, consisting of the coast plains and a strip of the table-land, nearly surrounding the state of Mysore and partly that of Hyderabad and the Central Provinces. It is conterminous with the provinces of Bengal and Bombay only for short distances. It lies between 8° 7′ (Cape Comorin) and 20° 25′

N. lat., and between 74° 41′ and 85° 13′ E. long., and extends 928 miles from north-north-east to south-south-west, and, where widest, 368 miles from east to west. It covers an area of nearly 150,000 square miles, or nearly one-fourth more than the whole area of the British Isles. But of this total, 9⅔ thousand square miles are native states feudatory to the Madras Government.

Hills and Rivers.—The Western Ghats, interrupted only for about 25 miles at the Pálghat gap, run parallel with the west coast, a distance of 420 miles within the presidency. They are a rugged escarpment of hard crystalline rocks, rising to over 7000 feet in the Nilgiris and Anaimalais. The Eastern Ghats are less uniform. To the north of the Godávari they consist of irregular groups of hills leading up to the table-land of Jeypore. Some peaks among them rise to nearly 5000 feet. A low range crosses the Godávari and Kistna a little above their deltas, and to the south of the former river becomes a series of parallel crescentic ranges of stratified rocks, including a broad plain between them. About 50 miles to the north-west of Madras these hills approach to within 30 miles of the coast, and from this point a better defined escarpment of crystalline rocks trends away to the south-west, bounding the state of Mysore and terminating in the Nilgiris. The Nilgiris rise into a little table-land of rolling grassy downs, with patches of forest in their depressions (Fig. 20), 20 miles across and between 6000 and 7000 feet above the sea, culminating in Dodabetta (8640 feet). The range south of the Pálghat gap rises to a similar but smaller table-land in the Anaimalais, the highest point of which, Anamudi (8840 feet), is the loftiest mountain in the peninsula. For 80 miles to the south of these run a series of less lofty plateaus, the Travancore hills, with an average width of 20 miles, and a narrower range continues nearly to Cape Comorin, terminating in Agastyamalai (6150 feet).

Several more or less detached hill groups, all of crystalline rocks, lie to the east of the ghat range, encroaching on the plain of the Carnatic. To the north-west of Madras are the Nagari hills, a conspicuous object in approaching Madras from the sea; and to the south-west are the

Javadi hills (3000 feet). Farther south are the Kalryenmalais (4000 feet), the Shevaroys (5410 feet), the Kolamalais (4663 feet), and the Pachaimalais (2500 feet), forming two great clusters to the north of Trichinopoly, separated only by the narrow Atúr Pass. And again to the south-west of Trichinopoly, the Serumalais (4000 feet), and to the west of them the Palnis (7000 feet), these last linked on to the Anaimalais.

All the great rivers of the peninsula south of the Tapti

FIG. 20.—THE NILGIRI TABLE-LAND AT SUNSET.

discharge on the east coast, and all but the Tapti and Mahánadi in Madras territory. The Godávari and Kistna have already been noticed under Hyderabad. Their deltas are contiguous for 20 miles inland from the coast, but between their upper portions the lake of Colar, 22 miles long and 8 broad, represents what was once a part of the sea, and has remained unfilled, the sediment of the rivers having been carried farther out and deposited beyond it. Both deltas project into the Bay of Bengal, and that of the Godávari protects the port of Cocanada, affording a safe anchorage in its roadstead in the south-west monsoon.

Proceeding southwards, the next large river is the

Pennér. This rises in the Nandidrug hills in the east of Mysore, flows northwards for 120 miles, then turns to the east and south-east, cutting through the triple range of the Eastern Ghats, and crossing the plain of Nellore, empties itself into the bay 18 miles below that town. Its total course is about 360 miles. The Corteliar, which debouches a few miles north of Madras, is a small river draining only the Nagari hills. The Pálár (milk river), to the south of Madras, is a larger stream. Its source is in the Mysore hills not far from that of the Pennér. It receives the drainage of the Eastern Ghats to the west of Madras and that of the Javadi hills, and flows past Arcot and Chingleput to the sea, near the old Dutch settlement of Sadras.

The next river, the Ponniár, is called the Púngani in Mysore, under which name it has already been noticed. Issuing from the Eastern Ghats it flows through the plain between the Kalryen and Javadi hills, and enters the sea by two mouths between Pondicherry and Cuddalore. The Vellár river rises in the Kalryenmalais (*malai* = hill), threads the Atúr Pass, and flows for 70 miles across the plain of the Carnatic to the sea at Porto Novo.

The Cauvery is the third in order of the great rivers of the Presidency. The main stream rises in Coorg, but its northernmost feeders are in the Bababudan hills in Mysore, and it receives the drainage of the whole range of the Western Ghats and the Nilgiris as far south as the Pálghat gap. Entering Mysore, it flows eastwards across the plateau which it serves to irrigate, washes the walls of Seringapatam 2338 feet above the sea, and in its passage through the Eastern Ghats, at Sivasamudram is precipitated over a magnificent fall 300 feet in height. It then turns southwards, for 90 miles winding through the hills of the Baramahál and across the plain between the Shevaroys and Nilgiris; and resuming its course eastwards, passes Trichinopoly. Above this town it sends off northwards its great branch the Coleroon, from which and from the main stream the rich district of Tanjore is fertilised by an elaborate system of annicuts and irrigation channels. The former enters the sea a little south of Porto Novo, the latter at Negapatam. The delta of the Cauvery is everywhere many feet above the sea level and along the sea-face is in places cut into a low cliff. It terminates on the south in Point Calimere. The total length of the Cauvery is 475 miles.

The largest river to the south of the Cauvery is the Vaigai, which rises in the eastern slopes of the Travancore hills, and crosses the dry plain of Tinnevelly to Palk's Bay. It enters the sea a few miles north of the remarkable projection of the mainland which, together with Rámeswaram island, Adam's Bridge, and Manaar island, nearly link Ceylon to India.

There are two lakes, or rather lagoons, of considerable size in the presidency, viz. the Colar lake, already mentioned above, and the Pulicat lake to the north of Madras, cut off from the sea by a sand spit, now covered with forest.

Administrative Divisions.—The fiscal subdivision of the Madras presidency differs from that of the northern provinces, in that the districts are generally larger and are not combined in divisions or commissionerships. They are twenty-two in number as follow:—

Districts.	Area. Sq. m.	Population.
Ganjam	8311	1,749,604
Vizagapatam	17,380	2,485,141
Godávari	7345	1,791,512
Kistna	8471	1,548,480
Nellore	8739	1,220,236
Cuddapah	8745	1,121,038
Kurnool	7788	709,305
Bellary } Anantapur }	11,007	1,336,696
Chingleput	2842	981,381
North Arcot	7256	1,817,814
South Arcot	4873	1,814,738
Tanjore	3654	2,130,383
Trichinopoly	3561	1,215,033
Madura	8401	2,168,680
Tinnevelly	5381	1,699,747
Salem	7653	1,599,595
Coimbatore	7842	1,657,690
Nilgiris	957	91,034
Malabar	5765	2,365,035
South Kanara	3902	959,514
Madras City	27	405,848

The two northernmost districts Ganjam and Vizagapatam are on the east coast north of the Godávari and include the coast plain and a considerable tract of the adjacent hill country. The Godávari and Kistna districts comprise the deltas of those rivers and the surrounding plain with the marginal portion of the Ghat range; the Nellore district all the coast plain to the south of the latter as far as the southern end of the Pulicat lake. The Cuddapah, Kurnool, and Anantapur districts the great stretch of country occupied by the triple Ghat range and the broad intervening valleys; and the Bellary district the more level ground of the plateau beyond. The small district of Chingleput is the plain around Madras extending from the Pulicat lake to about midway between Chingleput and Pondicherry; and the north Arcot district the remainder of the plain to the west together with the ghats and outlying hills, up to the borders of Mysore. South Arcot is the wide plain south of these districts as far as the Vellár and lower Coleroon; and Trichinopoly the remainder of the plain north of the Coleroon and Cauvery, and a small area to the south of the latter river. Tanjore occupies the rich delta tract and a strip of the coast to the south, and the remainder of the Carnatic plain is shared between Madura and Tinnevelly. The former of these also includes the Serumalais and Palni hills. Salem is a very hilly district, comprising all the country to the west of South Arcot and Trichinopoly down to the Cauvery, and on the north-west the Ghat range up to the borders of Mysore; and Coimbatore, the great dry plain between the Anaimalais, the Nilgiris, the Eastern Ghats, and the Cauvery, together with portions of the surrounding hills.

The districts of the west coast are,—South Kanara on the north adjoining Bombay, and Malabar on the south down to the border of the state of Cochin.

Native States.—There are five native states feudatory to the Madras government, the largest being Travancore at the south-western extremity of the peninsula. The Maharajah is of an ancient Hindu family of the Kshetrya caste, and the rulers have been long distinguished for their enlightenment. The observatory established by them at

Travancore has made valuable contributions to science. Cochin is a small state adjoining Travancore on the north. Pudukota is a wild jungly tract south of Tanjore and Trichinopoly. Banganapalle is a small state in the Eastern Ghats of Kurnool, well known from its diamond mines; and Sundúr another small hill tract to the west of Bellary. Their areas and population are respectively as follow :—

States.	Area Sq. m.	Population.
Travancore	6730	2,401,158
Cochin	1361	600,278
Pudukota	1101	302,127
Banganapalle	306	30,754
Sundúr	140	10,532

Madras City.—In population (406,000) and general importance Madras is the third city in India. It was established as the Factory of Fort St. George in 1639, earlier therefore than either Calcutta or Bombay, but having only an open roadstead, and no navigable river to bring down to it the produce of the country, its growth has been slower than that of the other presidency capitals. The fort is situated on the sea-shore, the Black Town, the commercial centre, to the north of it, and the suburbs extend around to the west and south at varying distances. It is the seat of government, of a university, and an astronomical observatory which affords the standard of longitude, and also the standard of civil time for the whole of India. A harbour has been formed by enclosing a portion of the roadstead with two breakwaters, constructed of blocks of concrete, but it is still a question how far this structure can withstand the destructive action of the cyclones that are very prevalent on this coast.

Other Towns, Ports, and important Places.—The second city in the presidency is Trichinopoly (84,500), at the head of the Cauvery delta, with a rock 273 feet high crowned with a temple, in the middle of the city; and on a neighbouring island in the Cauvery the great Vishnavaite temple of Sriringham (Fig. 21), with seven encircling walls, the outer two miles in circuit. Trichinopoly is an important military cantonment, and well known for its manufacture of cigars and the jewelry known as *swami* work. Tanjore (54,700), 32 miles to the east of Trichinopoly, is the ancient capital of the Chola kingdom, and in the last century that of a Maráthá dynasty; with one of the finest temples of Southern India. Madura (74,000), the Benares of Southern

FIG. 21.—THE SRIRINGHAM PAGODA, TRICHINOPOLY.

India, on the Vaigai river. It was the ancient capital of the Pandyan kings, and has a famous pagoda. Kumbakónum (50,000), in the Cauvery delta, a seat of Hindu learning, also with a fine pagoda. Bellary (53,500), in the north of the presidency, is a large military station with a rock fort. Arcot (12,000), though a small city, is historically famous for its defence by Clive, which was the turning-point of British ascendency in the Carnatic and India.

The principal minor ports on the east coast, chiefly frequented by coasting vessels, are in order from north to south: Gopalpur, Vizagapatam, Bimlipatam, Cocanada, Masulipatam, Negapatam, and Tuticorin; and on the west coast Mangalore, Beypore, and Cochin. Masulipatam (36,500), on the shore of the Kistna delta, is memorable as the site of the first British factory on the east coast of India. Tuticorin is a port for trade with Ceylon and the centre of the pearl and chank-shell fishery. The coffee of the Wynaad is exported from Beypore. Six miles distant is Calicut, which gives its name "calico" to cotton cloth.

The chief hill-station of Southern India is Ootacamund (7271 feet), on the Nilgiris. It is the summer seat of the Madras Government.

The most striking architectural productions of Southern India are the temples, which differ greatly from those of Northern India (compare, *e.g.*, Figs. 10 and 21). They are enclosed with high walls, sometimes of great circuit, as at Sriringham, and have the peculiarity that the entrance gate, termed the *goparam*, is often more conspicuous and elaborate than the shrine itself. Tanjore and Madura afford some of the finest examples. None are more than a few centuries old.

At Amrávati on the Kistna, north-west of Guntúr, is a fine example of an ancient Buddhist stone railing; and at Mahabalipuram, or the Seven Pagodas, on the sea-coast, near Sadras, are some remarkable sculptured caves of Brahminical origin of about the same period as those of Ellora, and monolithic temples carved in the solid rock. One of the latter is represented in Fig. 22.

Population.—The population of the Madras presidency in round figures is 34¼ millions, an average of 229 to the square mile, so that in density of population Madras ranks next after the North-West Provinces and Bengal. The most populous districts are Tanjore with 583 and South Kanara with 410 to the square mile, and the deltaic tracts of the Kistna and Godávari districts. The most thinly peopled are the arid districts of Kurnool with 91 and Coimbatore with 95 to the square mile.

The great mass of the people are Hindus, who constitute 92·3 per cent of the whole; the Muhammadans contribute only 6·2 per cent. There are a few Jains, and native Christians are proportionally more numerous than in any other province of India, numbering 1,346,000 or 1·7 per cent. In Travancore and Cochin they form one-fourth of the population. Among Hindus the worshippers of Shiva are more numerous than those of Vishnu in the proportion of 3 to 2, whereas in Northern India the latter

FIG. 22.—MONOLITH ROCK-CUT TEMPLE AT MAHABALIPURAM.

greatly preponderate. The population are largely of aboriginal descent; pariahs or outcastes constitute 15·6 per cent, but though so regarded by the higher castes, they rank themselves under more than 1000 sub-castes. A peculiar social feature of Southern India is the distinction of right and left hand castes, a distinction which is the source of great mutual jealousy and not infrequent disturbance. Each of these includes many different castes as dependent on race and occupation, and it is said that in

FIG. 23.—TODAS, ABORIGINALS OF THE NILGIRI HILLS.

certain cases the men belong to the left-hand and the women to the right-hand caste or *vice versâ*. Its origin is very obscure.

The aboriginal tribes who still live apart in the wilds of Southern India are restricted to the Western and Eastern Ghats, the Nilgiris, Anaimalais, and some other hill groups, and especially the hills north of the Godávari, bordering on the Central Provinces. In the Nilgiris alone are four such tribes, the most remarkable of whom are the Todas (Fig. 23). These differ strikingly in features and general appearance, especially in independence and dignity of bearing, from any other aboriginal race, and live in huts of a peculiar structure. Their origin is very obscure, and some have even supposed them to be of Celtic or Semitic descent, notwithstanding that their language is Dravidian. Among the aboriginals of the northern hills the Khonds, allied to the neighbouring Gonds, practised human sacrifices up to a late period.

Five languages are spoken in different parts of the presidency, not counting the aboriginal tongues; all are of the Dravidian class. These are Tamil in the Carnatic south of Nellore, and Telugu in the north, Canarese in the districts north of Mysore, Malayalum on the south-west coast, and Tulu in South Kanara.

Productions.—The southern presidency has no workable coal, and but few minerals of value except in small quantities. Gold occurs in the Wynaad, and diamonds are or have been obtained at several places in Cuddapah, Kurnool, and Bellary. These were the mines once famous as those of Golconda, but they are now but little worked. Aquamarines are found in Coimbatore, common amethysts in Trichinopoly, and corundum and chrome iron in Salem. Very rich and pure iron ores are abundant, and were at one time smelted by European processes at Porto Novo and Beypore, but the works were abandoned for the want of fuel.

Except wheat and barley, most Indian field crops are raised; cotton, indigo, sesamum or gingelly, and ground nuts largely for export. Pepper and cardamoms are grown in Travancore and Malabar, and cocoa-nuts all round the coast. The Wynaad and Nilgiris are the chief seat of coffee cultivation, and cinchona and tea are grown on the Nilgiris, the former extensively. Excellent cigars are manufactured both for home consumption and export from tobacco grown in Madura, Tanjore, Trichinopoly, and Godávari districts. The forests yield teak, red sanders, black-wood, satin-wood, ebony, sandal-wood, myrobolans, and cardamoms, and there is an important pearl and shell fishery at Tuticorin.

There are not many important manufactures. Fine cotton cloths and muslins were formerly one of the chief exports to Europe, especially from Masulipatam, and though the manufacture is greatly reduced, they are still produced both there, at Vizagapatam, Arni, and some other places. Trichinopoly is famous for its cigars and gold jewelry, Tanjore for ornamental work in copper and silver, and Vizagapatam for ornaments in horn and ivory.

Railways.—Starting from Madras, two railways, the Madras and South Indian Railways, communicate with the outlying districts and neighbouring states and presidencies. The Madras Railway runs west to Arconum and divides into two branches, viz. the north-western, which ascends the ghats north of Madras to Cuddapah and Gooty, and thence runs northwards into Hyderabad to meet the southern branch of the Great Indian Peninsular Railway from Bombay. At Guntakal, near Gooty, it is crossed by the Bellary and Kistna Railway, which runs westward to Bellary and then across the Kistna into Hyderabad and the southern districts of Bombay, and eastwards through the ghats to Nandyál, whence it is being continued to Guntúr and the Kistna opposite Bezváda; and the south-western branch, which runs down parallel with the Eastern Ghats to Salem and Coimbatore, and passes through the Pálghat gap to Beypore. A branch line runs to Bangalore and Mysore, another to Trichinopoly, where it meets the South Indian Railway, and a third from Coimbatore to the foot of the Nilgiris.

The South Indian Railway runs south to Chingleput and on to Cuddalore on the coast, with a short branch to Pondicherry. From Cuddalore it continues down the coast to Porto Novo and crosses the Cauvery delta to Tanjore, from which place a railway leads in one direction to Trichinopoly, in another to Negapatam on the coast. From Trichinopoly the railway runs south to Madura, Tinnevelly, and Tuticorin.

BURMA

Area, 280,000 square miles. Population, 8,700,000

Name and Government.—The British province of Burma (from Brahma) now includes the whole of the territories that in the beginning of this century were ruled by the house of Alompra from Ava, with the exception of Assam, which has been made an independent province. Up to 1887, Ava or Upper Burma with the tributary Shan States remained independent, while Arakan and Tenasserim, annexed to India in 1826, and Pegu in 1854, made up the province distinguished as British Burma. The whole is now again consolidated under a chief commissioner.

General Features.—Burma consists of—(1) a broad zone of wild and in great part unknown hills on the west, bordering the bay of Bengal, the Arakan Yoma, 170 miles broad in the north and tapering southwards to Cape Negrais; (2) the valleys of the Irawadi and its great tributary the Kyendwen or Chindwin; and (3) another great tract of hills and table-lands to the east of these, traversed from north to south by the Salween, and extending eastward beyond the valley of the Mekong or Cambodia river. The boundary between Burma and Yunan, which is at present somewhat indefinite, runs down through these hills as far as the Shwéli river, and then eastward across the Salween and the Cambodia river as far as the range that separates the feeders of the Cambodia river from those of the Red River of Tong King; returning westwards in about lat. 20° 30′ and again intersecting the Salween in lat. 20°. All the territory comprised in this great circuit consists of the Shan States tributary to Burma. Their geography is but little known, beyond the fact that they consist of an upland country intersected by hill ranges.

The Arakan Yoma consists of a great number of narrow parallel ridges running generally north and south and continuous with the hills of Manipur and Cachar. Between these ridges, the rivers that drain them run in straight rocky valleys, occasionally breaking across a ridge to effect a junction with a neighbouring stream, and are sometimes navigable by small boats for distances of many miles together between the rapids. All these hills are formed chiefly of sandstones, shales, and other soft stratified rocks of late geological age, that have been thrown up in parallel north and south folds which determine the direction of the ridges and valleys. They are generally covered with forest or dense bamboo jungle, and are tenanted by quite uncivilised tribes, much addicted to raiding. The Irawadi and Chindwin valleys are a series of plains intersected by ranges of low hills having the same characteristic direction and often confining the rivers in narrow defiles. Owing to the sparseness of the population of Burma, these plains, though naturally fertile and well supplied with water, are yet in great part uncultivated and still covered with forest. They form, however, but a small proportion of the total area.

Of the hills east of the Irawadi, the main ranges only run north and south, sending off spurs with a more or less transverse direction and spreading out into table-lands. They are partly formed of hard crystalline rocks, and in northern Burma and near its border in Yunan territory there are two extinct volcanoes, Popa and Hawshuenshan. These hills are occupied by several semi-civilised tribes,—Kachins in the north, in the neighbourhood of Bhamo, and Karennees north-east of Pegu, but chiefly by Shans. The range west of the Salween terminates on the south opposite Moulmein, where the river debouches on the Gulf of Martaban, but that to the east of the river continues down the Malay peninsula, of which it forms the backbone, dividing Tenasserim from the territory of Siam. The coasts of Arakan and Tenasserim are generally rocky and bordered by islands, which are the protruding summits of the coast ranges as they become successively submerged and disappear beneath the sea. The largest of these are Ramree island and Cheduba, off the coast of Arakan. On the Tenasserim coast, where the hills consist of hard rocks, both the coasts of the mainland and of the outlying islands present a bold precipitous face to the sea, but on the Arakan coast the rocks are softer and the coast is less bold and abrupt.

The summer monsoon blows directly and very strongly

on the Burmese coast, and up the valley of the Irawadi, and discharges a very heavy rainfall on Arakan and Tenasserim and the shores of Pegu. The rains begin in May and last till the end of October, longer therefore than in most parts of India, and the climate is consequently damp and the vegetation dense and luxuriant. But in the Irawadi valley this is the case only near the coast. On ascending the river the rainfall rapidly diminishes and the climate becomes drier, and in Ava up to Pagán, and even to Mandalay, it more nearly resembles that of the Carnatic. Still farther north, as the hills become more elevated, the climate is again damper, and in the extreme north it is more like that of Assam.

Owing to its hills, forests, and rivers, and the general richness of its vegetation, Burma is an extremely picturesque country by nature; and not less so are the dresses of the people, bright with many coloured silks, the *zayâts* and *khyoungs* (image houses and monasteries) with their richly carved woodwork, and the graceful pagodas, which, resplendent with gold, reflect the flash of the sun's rays like some distant pharos, or crown with their delicate, tapering pinnacles the eminences of the tree-clad hills.

Position and Area.—Before the annexation of Upper Burma, the area of the British territory as ascertained by survey was 87,220 square miles. The boundaries of Ava and the Shan States have not yet been demarcated, and their total area can only be roughly estimated at 192,000 square miles. That of the entire province may therefore be taken in round numbers at 280,000 square miles, which is considerably more than twice that of the British Isles, and one-third greater than that of the German Empire. Its northern limit may be taken as that of the Chindwin basin in 27° 20′ N. lat., its southernmost in lat. 10°, and its western and eastern as E. long. 92° 16′ and about 103° respectively. Its greatest length is therefore about 1160 miles, and its greatest width about 600 miles. On the west it is bounded by the Bay of Bengal and the Chittagong district of Bengal, on the north-west by Manipur and the Singpho territory of Assam, on the north-east by Yunan, on the east by Tong King, and on the south-east by Siam.

Mountains and Rivers.—The hill system of the Arakan Yoma is the southward extension of the ranges that bound Assam and Cachar on the east and those that bound Sylhet on the south. The main chain, to which alone the term Yoma is strictly applicable, is the continuation of that which divides the valleys of the Brahmaputra and the Barák from the Hukong valley of the Upper Chindwin and the valley of Manipur, and runs southward, rising in Sang Al Klang to 7438 feet and in Malselai Mon or Blue Mountain to 7100 feet. South of this last peak the range bends to south-south-east, dividing Arakan from Ava. Near the borders of Pegu and Ava, in lat. 19° 30′, it rises into several peaks between 4000 and 5000 feet, but declines farther south. Opposite Myanoung one peak rises to 4003 feet, but for the last 80 miles, before it terminates in Pagoda point at Cape Negrais, its height varies only between 200 and 400 feet.

To the east of the Irawadi valley in Pegu, the range termed the Pegu Yoma runs north and south between the Irawadi and the Sittang. This begins as a low ridge near Rangoon, and on the outskirts of the town is crowned with the great golden pagoda. As such it continues for 30 miles to the north, when it rises into a conspicuous hill range, and in the north of Pegu attains an altitude of 2000 feet, sinking again into the plains of southern Ava.

The next range to the eastward is more important. It runs southward uninterruptedly from the Himalaya, separating the eastern tributaries of the Irawadi from the Salween, and sending off branches that again ramify in the Kachin hills opposite Bhamo, and beyond Momien rise to 8000 feet; the hills above the ruby mines, north of Mandalay, which are equally high; and the Karennee hills, which rise to 9000 feet north-east of Pegu. East of the Sittang it bifurcates, throwing off the Poungloung range, which forms the eastern water-parting of the Sittang, and as a continuous range it terminates opposite Moulmein.

The next parallel range also runs down from the Himalaya and, as the Tanen Toung Gyi in the Shan States, divides the tributaries of the Salween from those of the Cambodia river. A range which rises parallel to this, but *en echelon*, farther west, runs southward between the Salween and the Meinam, and is continued down the Tenasserim peninsula under the name of the Tenasserim Yoma. Its greatest elevation in Tenasserim is about 5000 feet.

By far the most important river of Burma is the Irawadi. Its source is still unknown and has been the subject of much discussion among geographers. The main stream probably comes from Tibet, breaking through the eastern Himalaya, where it is known as the Lu-tse-Kyang or Lu river,[1] and it enters Upper Burma under the name of the Kewhom or Meh Kha, but this is known from native report only, in lat. 26°, where it unites with a smaller river, the Mali Kha, that comes from the north, and rises in the mountains that close the eastern end of the Assam valley. A little below lat. 25° where it receives the Mogoung river from the west, the Irawadi is a fine river, half a mile broad and from two to three fathoms deep, flowing at the rate of two miles an hour. Below this it enters the first defile, where at one place it is contracted by rocks to 70 yards in the dry season, and this defile continues to five miles above Bhamo. A second occurs below Bhamo, a third 40 miles above Mandalay, and a fourth between Thyetmyo and Prome. It receives several affluents from the east, the largest of which, the Shwéli, comes from Yunan and is navigable in the rainy season; but its greatest tributary is the Chindwin which joins it from the north-west, 58 miles below Mandalay. It enters its delta at Myanoung and gives off branches, one of which forms the Bassein river, a large navigable stream that enters the sea near Cape Negrais, and another communicates with the Rangoon river at the eastern extremity of the delta. The length of the Irawadi from the Kewhom in lat. 26° to the sea is 850 miles, all of which is navigable to boats. Steamers ascend it 700 miles to Bhamo.

The Chindwin rises below a peak 10,400 feet high, in lat. 27°, to the east of Upper Assam, under the name of the Turong Kha. It traverses the Hukong valley east of the Pátkai range, where it is navigable to boats, but

[1] This is the view advocated by General J. T. Walker, the late Surveyor-General of India.

from which it descends by rapids and a fall in lat. 26°. From this point, 300 miles above its junction with the Irawadi, it is again navigable to boats, and to steamers in the rainy season. It skirts the Nága hills, those that shut in the Kubo valley, and the ranges of the Arakan Yoma, receiving from them the Tuzu, the Yu river, and the Myittha (from Manipur), and from the mountains on the north-east, the Uru river. At Mengin it bends to south-south-east and unites with the Irawadi above Myingyan.

The next river of importance in point of size is the Salween, but flowing in a narrow valley hemmed in by mountains, and much obstructed by rocky barriers and rapids, it is navigable only for 80 miles from the sea. Like the Irawadi, its origin is unknown, and though some consider it to be the same as the Lu river from Tibet, the Jesuit missionaries, to whom we owe much of our knowledge of western China, place its sources in lat. 27° 10′, which is the more probable, as in lat. 25° it is a much smaller river than the Irawadi. It runs south through Yunan and the Shan States, afterwards forming the boundary between Burma and Siam, till, entering Tenasserim and passing Moulmein, it discharges itself into the Gulf of Martaban by two mouths separated by a hilly island.

Between the Irawadi and the Salween is the Sittang in Pegu. This rises in the hills around Yamèthin in Ava, drains the eastern slopes of the Pegu Yoma and the western slopes of the Karennee hills and the Poungloung, and discharges its waters into the head of the Gulf of Martaban. It is remarkable among all the rivers of India for the enormous bore or tidal wave, which at spring tides rolls up the lower part of its channel in a wave 20 feet high, rendering navigation impracticable from the sea. It can, however, be reached by boats from Rangoon, through the Pegu river and a canal.

In Arakan the largest river is the Kuladán, which rises in the Arakan Yoma, a few miles south of the Blue Mountain, and runs a nearly straight course southwards to Akyab, receiving the drainage of all the western half of the Yoma. It forms a delta of some size, which is the most productive part of Arakan, but is nearly enclosed by the hills of the mainland and the hilly Barongo islands opposite its mouth.

The province of Tenasserim is chiefly drained by three rivers, all of which flow in longitudinal valleys parallel with the coast and the Tenasserim Yoma. In the north the Attaran, which runs northward and enters the Salween just above Moulmein. Farther down, the Tavoy river, a small stream, which flows south, passes the town of that name, and ends in a long estuary shut off from the sea by the coast range of hills, and is navigable by small sea-going steamers up to Tavoy; and, in the south, the Tenasserim river, about 240 miles long, which also flows south and enters the sea at Mergui.

Adminstrative Divisions.—Lower Burma is administered under four divisions and nineteen districts; Upper Burma under four divisions and seventeen districts, in addition to which the uncivilised Yau and Chin hill country, and the northern and southern Shan States are separate political charges. The areas and population of only the districts of Lower Burma can be given.

LOWER BURMA

Divisions.	Districts.	Area. Sq. m.	Population.
Arakan	Akyab	5,535	359,706
	North Arakan	1,015	14,499
	Kyouk-pyoo	4,309	149,303
	Sandoway	3,667	64,010
Pegu	Rangoon town	22	134,176
	Hanthawaddy	4,236	427,720
	Tharrawaddy	2,014	278,155
	Prome	2,887	322,342
Irawadi	Thonegwa	5,413	284,063
	Bassein	7,047	389,419
	Henzada	1,948	318,077
	Thyetmyo	2,397	169,560
Tenasserim	Moulmein town	14	53,107
	Amherst	15,189	301,086
	Tavoy	7,150	84,988
	Mergui	7,810	56,559
	Shwaygyin	5,567	171,144
	Toungoo	6,354	128,848
	Salween	4,646	30,009

UPPER BURMA

Divisions.	Districts.	Divisions.	Districts.
Northern	Mandalay. Bhamo. Myadaung. Ruby mines. Shwebo. Ye-u.	Central	Sagaing. Kyaukse. Lower Chindwin. Upper Chindwin. Myingyan.
Southern	Pagan. Minbu. Taungdwingyi.	Eastern	Meiktila. Yamèthin. Pyinmana.

Towns, etc.—Rangoon (134,000), the present capital of Burma, is situated 21 miles from the sea on the Rangoon river, at the junction of the Hlaing and Pegu rivers, and communicating by a navigable creek with the Irawadi. As a port it nearly rivals Madras in the amount of its commerce, and will probably surpass it before long. The Shwé (Golden) Dagon pagoda 320 feet high and gilt from base to summit (Fig. 24), which crowns the low ridge north of the town, is the most venerated shrine in Burma. It is believed to cover four hairs and certain other relics of Buddha Gautama. The chief local industry is that of the rice-husking mills, rice and teak timber being the principal articles of export. Moulmein (53,000), in Tenasserim, most picturesquely situated on the Salween below its junction with the Attaran, and at the bifurcation of its two estuarine outlets. Founded since the British occupation of the province. It is the chief entrepôt of the trade in teak timber, which is floated down from the forests by the Salween and Attaran rivers. Akyab (34,000), the chief port of Arakan, at the mouth of the Kuladán river; also founded since the British occupation. Mandalay (65,000), the late royal capital of Upper Burma or Ava, on the left bank of the Irawadi, surrounded by a square walled enclosure, one mile each way, and containing within a separate enclosure the palace of the late king. The city was founded only about thirty years ago, the older capitals, Amarapura and Ava, being somewhat lower down the river. The still older mediæval capital, Pagán (from the ninth to the thirteenth century), on the left bank of the Irawadi, 80 miles below Mandalay, covers with its ruins a space of 16 square miles. Its temples, estimated

FIG. 24.—THE SHWÉ DAGON PAGODA, RANGOON.

by Sir Henry Yule to number 800 or 1000, are many of them of a different type from the *stupas* of modern Burma or from any Indian edifice. The finest of them, the

Ananda (Fig. 25), a solid mass of brickwork 200 feet square and 168 feet high, is still kept in repair. It is said to have been built about the time of the Norman conquest of England.

Other important places are—Bhamo, on the left bank of the Irawadi, 200 miles above Mandalay, a stockaded

FIG. 25.—THE ANANDA, PAGÁN.

town, the terminus of steamer navigation and the starting-point of the trade route to China. Prome (29,000), the capital of the former kingdom of Prome, also on the left bank of the Irawadi, above the head of its delta, the terminus of a railway from Rangoon. Bassein (28,000), on the Bassein river, the most westerly arm of the Irawadi, a port visited by sea-going steamers. Minor ports are Sandoway and Kyouk-pyoo in Arakan, and Tavoy and Mergui in Tenasserim.

Population.—According to the census of 1881, the population of Lower Burma was $3\frac{3}{4}$ millions. That of

Upper Burma was estimated in 1886 at 3 millions, and that of the tributary Shan States at 2 millions. This gives an average of only 43 to the square mile in Lower Burma, and less than 24 to the square mile in Upper

FIG. 26.—BURMESE GENTLEMAN AND LADY.

Burma and the Shan States. It is true that a large proportion of the country is hilly; but even the fertile plains are very thinly peopled, and large tracts of excellent culturable land are still waste. Hence the Burmese are in much easier circumstances than the people of India, and are increasing at the rate of 4 per cent per annum. The immigration from India, chiefly from Madras, amounted in 1886 to 56,000, but as 51,000 returned in the same year, the increase of population from this source is but small.

All the natives of Burma are of Indo-Chinese race, with perhaps a partial exception in the case of the Mon or Talaings of Pegu and Arakan, who are believed to be in part descended from immigrants from the coasts of Madras (Telingána) in the early centuries of our era. Another race distinct from the Burmese, the Karens, numbering $\frac{3}{4}$ million, are found only in Pegu. The plains of Ava are peopled solely by Burmese (Fig. 26) and some Shans, but the bulk of the Shans occupy the hill states to the east of the Irawadi, partly tributary to Burma, partly to China, and partly to Siam. Except the Karens, all these are Buddhists, but in the religion of the lower classes there remains much of the original belief in spirits (*nâts*) and demons (*bilus*), who have to be propitiated by offerings. The Karens are nature worshippers, but of the 84,000 Christians returned in the census a larger proportion are of this race. Hindu settlers and immigrants amount to 88,000, and except among them there are no caste divisions in Burma. Chinese are numerous in Rangoon and Moulmein, and other sea-ports.

Of the hill people, the Shans of the eastern hills have already been mentioned. Another race inhabiting a part of the northern Shan country is the Paloungs, a quiet, retiring race, who collect and prepare the indigenous tea of those hills. The hills to the north-east of Pegu are occupied by the Karennees or red Karens, a warlike and courageous race, who have always been friendly to the British. The hills to the north of Bhamo and about the sources of the Chindwin, up to the Assam frontier, are inhabited by Kachins or Singphos, and those to the west of the Chindwin by Chins of various tribes, who tattoo the faces of their women. These last are very predatory in their habits, raiding on each other and the people of the plains for slaves and heads, and their pacification and subjection is a part of the work now in progress. These various wild tribes of the north and west are estimated at $\frac{3}{4}$ million.

Productions.—Among the most valuable mineral products of Burma are rubies, which are almost a monopoly of Burma, the mines being situated in the hills north of Mandalay. In the hills farther north, near Mogoung, are the famous jade mines, that supply this much-prized stone to China; and amber mines exist still farther north. Petroleum, known as Rangoon oil, has long been obtained from wells in the Irawadi valley near Yenangyoung, and coal is worked on the Chindwin. Another coalfield is known to exist close to the railway from Rangoon to Mandalay, and a third on the Irawadi between Mandalay and Bhamo. Tin is worked in Tenasserim, and there are quarries of fine white statuary marble near Mandalay.

But the chief productions of Burma at present are rice, teak timber, and fish, the latter for local consumption, chiefly in the form of *ngapi*, a highly odorous preparation of salted fish, in general use as a condiment. Burma now supplies the world with teak, and under a proper system of forest conservancy which is now being introduced, it is believed that the supplies of this most valuable timber may be rendered inexhaustible. Rice is grown on six-sevenths of the cultivated land of Lower Burma, and its export in 1886 amounted to about six millions sterling. The value of the fisheries in Lower Burma is estimated at one million sterling. Other articles of produce are cotton, which is exported to Yunan, india-rubber from the hills in the north of Ava, and wild tea from the Shan States, which is pickled and fermented for consumption as a condiment. There are also many excellent kinds of timber besides teak, one of which, padouk, is already in some demand. The Shans produce the finest breed of ponies known in any part of the Indian Empire.

The chief manufactures of Burma are silks, which are worn by all but the poorer classes, and cigars; light boxes of lacquered basket-work, known as Burma boxes; wood-carving, in which the Burmese excel; gongs, and embossed silver ware.

Railways.—There are already two railways in Burma: one from Rangoon to Prome on the Irawadi, and one up the Sittang valley to Toungoo and on to Mandalay. As there are but few roads in Burma, and districts at a distance from the Irawadi and the Chindwin have hitherto been but little accessible, it is probable that the railway system will be much extended in the course of a few years.

Andaman and Nicobar Islands

Area, 3285 square miles. Population, 30,000

General Features.—The Andaman and Nicobar islands are two groups forming part of a chain of islands

Fig. 27.—Barren Island.

that extend in a curved line between Cape Negrais and the northern extremity of Sumatra, and may be regarded as the emerging summits of a submarine range of hills linking the Arakan Yoma to the central hill range of Sumatra. They are formed of similar rocks, and are both groups of hilly islands surrounded with mangrove swamps and coral reefs. They are for the most part covered with forest, but in the Nicobars there are large tracts, the dense clay soil of which is unfavourable to vegetation, and these constitute grassy plains bare of forest.

The Andaman group consists of the Great Andaman, really a chain of four islands separated only by narrow creeks, 156 miles long and from 14 to 16 miles across;

the Little Andaman 34 miles to the south and 28 miles long, and a few smaller islands. Seventy and 80 miles to the east of the Great Andaman are two small islands, Narcondam and Barren Island (Fig. 27), that are isolated volcanoes, the former extinct, and the latter dormant since the first years of this century; both uninhabited.

The Nicobar islands lie 88 miles to the south of the Little Andaman, and extend for 170 miles in the direction of Sumatra. The group consists of eighteen islands, the largest of which, Great Nicobar, is 31 miles long and 14 across.

The Andaman islands were occupied by the British Government in 1858 for the purpose of establishing a penal settlement, and the Nicobars a few years later. Two such settlements have been formed, one at Port Blair in the Great Andaman, and one at Nancowry in the Nicobars. These settlements are under a superintendent and chief commissioner. The remainder of the islands is still occupied by the native aboriginals.

Position and Area.—The total area of the islands is 3285 miles, of which the Great Andaman constitutes two-thirds. The Andamans lie between 13° 40′ and 10° 25′, and the Nicobars between 9° 15′ and 6° 45′ N. lat., all between 92° and 94° E. long.

Port Blair.—The chief settlement is named after an officer of the Indian navy who first surveyed these islands in 1789, and endeavoured to colonise them. It is situated on a land-locked inlet on the east coast of the southern division of the Great Andaman. The Chief Commissioner and most of the European officers have their houses on a small island, Ross Island, at the entrance, and the convicts are established partly on this and other islets, partly on the shores of the inlet, which extends $7\frac{1}{2}$ miles into the interior. There is also a settlement, Port Mouat, on the opposite coast.

Aboriginal Population. — The native Andaman islanders, termed Mincopie, are of negrito race (see Fig. 3), very dark in skin tint, with rounded skulls and hair in small crisp curly knots. They are among the least advanced of mankind. Their dwellings are rudely put together with a few sticks and palm leaves, they wear no clothing beyond paint and a few twisted fibres, and have no arts except the manufacture of bows and arrows, baskets, mats, and canoes. They are not, as was once supposed, cannibals, but live on fish, which they catch by hand or shoot, on the wild pigs, a small species of which is indigenous to the islands, and on the roots and wild fruits of the forests. All refuse is thrown on a heap, and when this becomes too offensive the site is abandoned.

The Nicobars contain two distinct races. The people of the coasts are of Malay origin. They build their houses on piles, but they practise but little agriculture and live chiefly by fishing. In the interior of the islands there is a distinct race, the Shombengs, who have Mongol features and straight hair; they build small huts, cook their food in pots made of bark, and cultivate yams, plantains, and perhaps other kinds of garden produce. Of these people but little is known at present.

CEYLON

Area, 25,365 square miles. Population, 2,763,984

Name and Government.—Ceylon (Sinhala, the land of the lion), the Taprobane (Tambapáni, copper water) of the Macedonians, the Lanka dwipa (resplendent island) of the Hindus, and the Serendib (Sinhala dwipa) of the Arabs, is geographically and historically an appendage of India, and at some remote epoch was doubtless continuous with the mainland, but it presents such differences in its indigenous plants and animals that the separation must have taken place long prior to the reach of tradition; and at the present time, although British, it is a crown colony, independent of the government of India. At the head of its Government is a governor, appointed by the Colonial Office, with an executive council of five members, and a legislative council for enacting local laws.

General Features.—The island, which has somewhat the form of a pear, consists of a central mass of mountains comparable with some of the outlying hill groups of the Carnatic, and an encircling plain which occupies all the northern half of the island, and is narrower and more hilly on the east, west, and south. As in the Carnatic, the hills and plains consist of hard crystalline rocks, sometimes covered with laterite[1] (locally termed *cabook*), with a small fringe of recent marine formation, chiefly at its northern extremity.

The south-west of the island has a very damp and uniformly warm climate; at Point de Galle there is a difference of only 19° between the warmest day and the coldest night in the year. This dampness, arising from the frequency and heaviness of the rainfall, is caused by the hills which obstruct the currents of both the summer and winter monsoons from the opposite coasts. But the north-west and south-east coasts are very dry, and like the drier parts of the Carnatic. The vegetation shows corresponding differences. It is very dense and luxuriant on the hills and in the South-West Province from Galle to Colombo; less so to the east of the hills and over the northern plain; but the greater part of this plain is or was not many years ago covered with magnificent forest, in which lay hidden the ruins of great cities and tanks constructed by the native dynasties that ruled Ceylon from the fourth century B.C. and in the first twelve centuries of our era, before the country had been overrun and devastated by Indian invaders from the Madras coast.

Position and Area.—Ceylon lies between 5° 55′ and 9° 51′ N. lat. and between 79° 41′ and 81° 55′ E. long., and is 268 miles in length in a nearly north and south direction, and 144 miles across where widest. It covers an area of 25,365 square miles, and is more than three-fourths the size of Ireland.

Mountains and Rivers.—The mountains of Ceylon consist of a compact group occupying the central portion of the southern half of the island; and to the south-west a lower range running north-west and south-east nearer the coast. An irregular ridge also runs off to the north-east terminating near Batticaloa. All the country to the south-west and to the east of the central group is more or less

[1] A ferruginous clay, formed by the decomposition of felspathic and basaltic rocks, which hardens on long exposure to the atmosphere; very common in India.

hilly, and there are a few low hills to the north. The central group is highest on the south, when it culminates in the Horton plains, adjacent to which Kirigalpota and Totapelakanda rise to altitudes of 7832 and 7746 feet respectively. From the Horton plains a high ridge runs northward through the middle of the hills, in which Pidurutalagala reaches to 8296 feet, being the highest mountain in the island. Better known, however, than any of these is Adam's Peak, which rises boldly at the south-western corner of the central group to a height of 7353 feet. The summit is a place of pilgrimage equally to Buddhists, Muhammadans, and Hindus, a mark on the rock, regarded as a footprint, being variously attributed to Buddha, Adam, and Ráma.

The island is not large enough to allow of the formation of any large river. The largest is the Mahaweli Ganga, which rises under Pidurutalagala and flows past Kandy; then descending to the east of the hills it turns north and discharges itself by two mouths on the east coast; the most northerly enters the Bay of Trincomalee. It has a course of 134 miles and is navigable to small boats nearly up to Kandy. The other rivers are mere mountain torrents or otherwise of little importance.

Administrative Divisions.—The island is subdivided into seven provinces, the names, areas, and population of which are respectively as follow :—

Provinces.	Area. Sq. m.	Population.	Provinces.	Area. Sq. m.	Population.
Western .	3456½	897,329	Northern .	3171	302,500
North-Western	3024½	293,327	Central . .	6028¾	639,361
Southern .	1980	433,520	North-Central	4046¾	66,146
Eastern . .	3657½	127,555			

The provinces are further subdivided into 22 districts, varying from the municipality of Colombo with 9½ square miles to the single district of the thinly inhabited North-Central Province of 4046 square miles.

Towns, etc.—Colombo (110,500) the capital and seat of government, and also the chief port, situated on the west coast. Its harbour, constructed by enclosing a portion of the roadstead with a stone breakwater, and by dredging, is a port of call for the mail steamers *en route* to Calcutta, China, and Australia. Kandy (22,000), the latest capital of the native rulers of the island, is on the hills 72 miles from Colombo, 2000 feet above the sea. It is beautifully situated on a bend of the Mahaweli Ganga and on the bank of a small artificial lake. In one of its Buddhist temples is preserved a piece of ivory reputed to be a tooth of Buddha Gautama (the sacred *Delada*), but really a substitute for the original relic, which was destroyed by the Portuguese. Three miles from Kandy is the beautiful botanic garden of Peradeniya (see Fig. 2). Galle (33,000), at the south-western extremity of the island, 72 miles south of Colombo, an old Dutch fortified town with a small land-locked harbour, formerly the port of call for mail steamers. Jaffna (40,000), at the northern extremity of the island, an ancient Tamil settlement with a small Dutch fort. Trincomallee (10,000), on the north-east coast, with a fine natural harbour, the best in the island, now a coaling station for the British navy. Newara Eliya, at 6240 feet on the west flank of Pidurutalagala, is the hill sanitarium of the island. It has a cool climate, but owing to its exposed position it is so damp and rainy that except in the early spring months, before the setting in of the summer monsoon, it is but little resorted to.

The ancient native capital of Anarajapura and the mediæval capital of Pollanarua are now ruins buried in the seclusion of the northern forests.

Population.—The census of 1881 gave the total population of the island as rather more than 2¾ millions, being an average of 109 to the square mile. The most densely peopled province is the western, including Colombo and the adjacent coast, and the damp hilly country to the west and south of Adam's Peak, where the average is 260 to the square mile; and the most thinly populated, the North Central Province, the comparatively dry and rocky tract to the north of the hills, where there are only 16 to the square mile. The Sinhalese proper, nearly all Buddhists by religion, formed 67 per cent of the whole. They are chiefly restricted to the west and south of the island. Next in importance are the Tamils, chiefly Hindus from Southern India, who occupy most of the north and east, and are especially numerous as garden labourers on the plantations of the hills. They contribute 25 per cent. The Moormen of the coast, Muhammadans probably of mixed Arab descent, amount to 7 per cent, and the Eurasians and Burghers of mixed European descent and Christians, to 0·6 per cent. Europeans, including the civil officers of government and planters but not the military nor the seamen in the ports, were nearly 5000 in 1881. The aboriginal Veddahs (perhaps allied to the Beders of Mysore), a wild forest race restricted to the eastern jungles, numbered only 2228.

Productions.—The chief mineral productions are plumbago and gems. The latter, obtained from gravel pits at Ratnapura (jewel city) at the base of Adam's Peak, include sapphires, rubies, spinels, cinnamon stones and some other varieties of garnet, zircons, cats'-eyes, moonstones, and a few others. Up to within the last ten years the chief produce of the plantations was coffee, though it had been declining since 1870, when the fungus which has ruined the industry first became formidable. Tea has taken its place within the last few years, together with cinchona bark and cocao. Other important articles of export are cocoa-nut oil and *copra* (dried cocoa-nut), *coir* (cocoa-nut fibre), cinnamon, which grows wild in the forests, cinnamon oil, cardamoms, vanilla, citronella oil, ebony, sapan wood, and orchella weed. Excellent tobacco is grown around Jaffna, and the pearl fisheries of Manaar are an important source of revenue. Tortoise-shell is obtained on the coasts, and manufactured by the Sinhalese into combs, which are universally worn by the men as well as women.

Railways.—Colombo and Kandy are connected by a railway 74½ miles long, which ascends the hills by the Kaduganawa pass. From Kandy a line of 17½ miles carries on the communication northwards to Matale, and another of 17 miles southwards up the valley of the Mahaweli Ganga to Nawalapitya. Another railway from Colombo runs southward along the coast to Kaltura and Bentotte.

FOREIGN POSSESSIONS IN INDIA

FRANCE and Portugal are the only foreign nations that retain any possessions in India. The former has five settlements, viz. Pondicherry and Karikal on the coast south of Madras, Mahé on the west coast a few miles south of Tellicherry, Yanaon at the mouth of the Godávari, and Chandernagore in Bengal, on the Hooghly, 20 miles above Calcutta. The total area of these possessions is 178 square miles, and their population 280,300.

Of this total, the territory of Pondicherry alone occupies 133 square miles, and its governor is governor-general of the French possessions. Pondicherry consists of a white and black town. The former faces the sea, the better class of houses being built on the model of the town houses of France, surrounding a courtyard and opening by a *porte cochère* on the street. It has an open roadstead and an iron pier, and communicates with Madras by a branch railway, 24 miles long, to Villanur on the South Indian Railway. The Messagerie steamers call here *en route* for Madras and Calcutta.

The Portuguese settlements have a total area of 1096 square miles, and a population of 407,700. They are three in number, viz. Goa, Daman, and Diu, all on the west coast. The territory of Goa alone occupies 1062 square miles. It is situated between 14° 51′ and 15° 46′ N. lat., immediately north of the port of Karwar, and between 73° 44′ and 74° 24′ E. long. It extends 64 miles from north to south and 44 miles from east to west. It is a portion of the hilly tract between the crest of the Western Ghats and the sea, and includes the estuary of the Mandavi river, on which the city of Goa is situated, and also Marmugao bay, where a breakwater has been constructed affording protection to the anchorage. A railway from Sairuli at the crest of the ghats terminates here.

The capital city of Goa consists of the new and old cities, the former being the seat of the Government, the latter the ecclesiastical capital, with a fine old cathedral and the church of Bom Jesus, in which is preserved the body of Francis Xavier, the great apostle of India.

The small settlement of Daman is on the coast north of Bombay, and that of Diu in the Kattywar peninsula.

FRONTIER STATES

THE countries immediately surrounding India, Burma, and the tributary states included in the British Indian Empire are—on the west, Persia, adjacent to the western boundary of Balúchistán; Afghánistán, which bounds Balúchistán on the north and lies to the west of the Punjab, the hills between being occupied by independent Afghán or Pathán tribes, who have only recently been brought under the protection of the British Government; on the north-west, adjoining Hazára and Kashmír, the petty republics of Chilás and independent states of Yagistán; on the north Káshghár or Chinese Turkestan, and the Rudok and Nari Khorsum or Hundesh provinces of Tibet, as far east as the Sárda river, beyond which the Himalayan state of Nepal intervenes for 500 miles. Then to the north and east of the protected state of Sikkim, Tibet again bounds British India. To the north of Assam the frontier is partly contiguous with Bhotan, partly with the territories of the Akas, Daphlas, and other independent hill tribes. Other tribes, the Mishmis, Kamptis, and Singphos, occupy the mountains east of Assam and north of Burma. On the north-east of Burma the Chinese province of Yunan is conterminous with the British frontier, which is not yet demarcated, and extends along the north of the tributary Shan states, which stretch eastwards to Tong King. Lastly, Siam bounds these states on the south and the British division of Tenasserim on the east.

Only two of these, viz. Afghánistán and Nepal, are so nearly connected with India as to need a more special description here.

AFGHÁNISTÁN

Name and Government.—Afghánistán (the land of the Afgháns), though not a part of British India, has been more than once under the same native dominion as North-Western India, and is now under British protection with reference to foreign countries. Its geographical position on the north-west frontier, and the fact of its being traversed by the only practicable routes leading to India from Persia and Central Asia, render its relations to India of very great importance. It is under the rule of the Amír of Kabul, whose government is despotic.

General Features.—It occupies most of the north-eastern part of the table-land of Irán, having Persia on the west and Balúchistán on the south. On the north the table-land is bounded by the Hindú Kúsh, the Koh-i-Baba, the Kúren and Kopet ranges and the Albúrz, of which the first two are included in Afghánistán; but the Amír's territory does not include the mountain ranges north of the Kabul river, which are occupied by independent tribes, while it does comprehend the northern spurs of the main mountain chain and the plain at their northern foot up to the Oxus river. The whole country is elevated; Kabul, the capital, being 5760 feet above the sea, Ghazni farther south 7280 feet, and Kandahár on the southern plain of the Arghandab 3350 feet. The most fertile parts are the series of plains traversed by the Kabul river, the southern plain around Kandahár watered by the Arghandab and other tributaries of the Helmand, the Hari Rúd valley around Herát, and the valley of the Oxus. All the remainder of the country is mountainous. The climate is dry, the summer monsoon rains of India hardly reaching to Afghánistán, so that cultivation is chiefly dependent on the winter and spring snowfall on the mountains, which feeds the rivers through the summer and affords water for irrigation.

Position and Extent.—The Amír's territory lies between 38° 25′ and about 30° N. lat., and between 60° 40′ and about 74° E. long., and extends 450 miles from north to south and 750 miles from east to west. Its area may be estimated in round figures as about 300,000 square miles. It has Persia on the west, the Russian Turkoman country and Bukhára on the north, Káshghár, Káfiristán and other independent hill territory on the north-east, the independent Afghán tribes under British protection on the east, and Balúchistán on the south.

Mountains and Rivers.—The principal mountain range is the Hindú Kúsh, which commences at the junction of the Kárákoram range of Kashmír with the Pamír table-land, in lat. 37°, and runs south-west a distance of 350 miles, with peaks rising to between 20,000 and 25,000 feet, and passes all over 12,000 feet. The Bamian Pass, west of Kabul, is the chief military route leading to the plains of the Oxus. To the west of this pass the range is lower, and under the name of the Koh-i-Baba runs westward, dividing about the meridian of 67° into three branches, enclosing the valleys of the Hari Rúd and Murghab rivers. The two southern branches, the Safed Koh (white mountain) and the Siah Koh (black mountain), continue west as far as Herát; the northern, though interrupted by the passage of the Murghab and Hari Rúd, may be considered as continued to the Caspian in the Kúren and Kopet ranges which bound the Persian plateau on the north, and beyond the Caspian, rise again in the great range of the Caucasus.

From the Hindú Kúsh and the Koh-i-Baba a series of parallel ranges run to the south-west between the former range and the Indus, and through the greater part of Afghánistán, enclosing the valleys of the Swát river, the Kunar, and other tributaries of the Kabul river, and farther west, the Lora, Tarnak, Arghandab, and the Helmand, all of which unite, and after a great bend to the south, terminate in the swampy lake of Sistán. The Farah and Hárút, still farther west, discharge into the same lake.

To the south of the Kabul river, the ranges running south-west from the Hindú Kúsh are crossed by a great range running nearly east and west, the Safed Koh (white mountains), the highest peak of which, Sítarám, reaches to 15,620 feet above the sea. The range is continued east into the Punjab, in the Afrídi and Jowáki hills, to the banks of the Indus. The Safed Koh divides the drainage basin of the Kabul river from that of the Kurram, another tributary of the Indus, and the Paghmán range running south-west separates the former from that of the Helmand.

The most important rivers of the table-land are the Kabul river and the Helmand; and those to the north of the Hindú Kúsh and Koh-i-Baba, the Oxus with its tributary the Panjah, both of which rise on the Pamír and flow westward, and the Murghab and Hari Rúd, which drain the Safed Koh and the Siah Koh, and, turning northward, lose themselves in the desert.

Towns.—Kabul, the capital, is situated on the right bank of the Kabul river, 5760 feet above the sea, and 190 miles west by north from Pesháwar. It is surrounded by mountains, except on the north-east. It was first made the capital of the country by the emperor Baber, whose tomb lies one mile to the west of the city. It is estimated to contain between 50,000 and 60,000 inhabitants. Kandahár, situated on a richly cultivated plain between the Arghandab and the Tarnak rivers, commanding a pass, through which lies the road to Herát. It is 370 miles from Herát, 110 miles from Pishín, the British frontier post near the present terminus of the Balúchistán Railway, and 315 from Kabul. It is a walled city of rectangular form, three and three quarter miles in circuit, with a population of about 30,000. Herát, often called the key of India, is a very ancient city in the valley of the Hari Rúd, 2650 feet above the sea, and is surrounded by 400 square miles of cultivated land. It is of square form, surrounded by a wall on the summit of an earthwork 50 feet high and four miles in circuit. Its population has varied at different times between 6000 or 7000 only and 100,000, and is now estimated at between 20,000 and 30,000. The road from Persia to Kandahár passes by Herát, and the valley of the Hari Rúd offers also easy access from Merv and Sarakhs. Ghazni, a fortified city commanding the road from Kandahár to Kabul, situated at the head of the Tarnak valley, 7280 feet above the sea. On the Túrkestán plain, between the Hindú Kúsh and the Oxus, the most famous city historically is Bálkh, the ancient Bactra, now in ruins.

Population.—The population of Afghánistán is estimated at 4,109,000, all Muhammadans, with the exception of a few Hindu settlers from India. The Afgháns, forming only 2½ per cent of the population, occupy most of the country to the east of the Paghmán range, and consist of four tribes, viz. the Duranis, to which belongs the family of the Amír, the Ghilzais, the Kakars, and the Yusafzais, who are independent of the Amír and occupy the hills north of Pesháwar and the plain at their foot. The hill country to the west of the Paghmán range is peopled by Hazáras, a race of Mongol origin; and the plain of Afghán Túrkestán chiefly by Usbeks, a confederation of various Tartar tribes. Tajíks, allied to Persians, are distributed throughout the country. The Afghán language, termed Pushtu, is an Aryan tongue.

Productions.—A valuable coalfield, at present unworked, exists in Afghán Túrkestán between Bálkh and Bamian. Gold, silver, copper, lead, and antimony are obtained to some extent, and the two latter occur at many places in Afghánistán. Among precious stones, chrysolites are found in Kandahár and lapis lazuli in Badakshán. Forests exist only on the higher mountains, consisting of deodars and various pines. The lower hills are bare of trees. Assafœtida grows wild and is largely collected. Fruits, such as apples, grapes, apricots, melons, pistachios, and pomegranates, are extensively cultivated and carried by Afghán traders, termed *povindas*, to all parts of India. Other exports are horses, wool, silk, madder, and assafœtida. There are but few manufactures. Herát is famous for carpets, and the sheepskin coats, termed *poshtins*, are an increasing article of trade.

Nepal

Government.—Nepal is an independent state under the nominal rule of a Rájput prince of the Sesodia clan. But the government is practically administered by the prime minister, a brother of the late Jung Bahadoor. The British Government is represented by a resident, and, excepting the officers of his staff, no other European is allowed to enter the country without special permission. Hence, excepting the valley of Kathmandu, the country, which is nearly all mountainous, is but little known in detail.

General Features.—The state consists of a length of about 500 miles of the Himalaya north of Oudh, the North-West Provinces, and Bengal, and of the strip of plain at its foot. The general character of the mountains is such as has already been described under the North-West Provinces and Bengal, viz. a range of towering peaks separated from each other by the valleys of the great rivers that drain their northern slopes, and forming the great snowy range. The main Tibetan range, farther north, that divides the basins of these rivers from that of the Sangpo or Upper Brahmaputra, is of less extreme altitude but uninterrupted. The secondary ranges, running north and south from the great peaks, uniting them with the Tibetan range, divide the country into three great valley systems belonging respectively to the drainage basins of the Gogra, the Gandak (Gunduk), and the Kosi (Koosee), a smaller tract on the extreme west draining into the Sárda, and two others entirely to the south of the great snowy range; one south of Dhaulagiri, forming the upper basin of the Rapti, the other, which includes the valley of Kathmandu, drained by a number of smaller rivers, most of which, after traversing the plain of Northern Behar, eventually unite in the Bur Gunduk.

The valley of Kathmandu is, on a much smaller scale, a repetition of the vale of Kashmír, viz. the bed of an ancient lake, 20 miles long and 15 broad, and about 4500 feet above the sea. This is the most highly cultivated and thickly populated part of the state. The Terái or plain at the foot of the Himalaya, if cleared, would furnish an extensive tract of arable land, but it is now chiefly swamp and forest, thinly peopled by a number of aboriginal tribes.

The climate of Nepal, like that of the Himalaya generally, is damp and cool on the hills, damp and hot in the narrow valleys south of the great snowy range, but more moderate in the high open valley of Kathmandu. To the north of the great snowy range it is much drier and more approaching that of Tibet.

Position and Extent.—Nepal lies between the meridians of 80° 10′ and 88° 15′ E. long., and between 26° 20′ and 30° 20′ N. lat. It extends 500 miles in a nearly east and west direction, with a breadth of between 90 and 140 miles in a north and south direction. Its area may be estimated at about 55,000 square miles, the same as that of Assam.

Mountains and Rivers.—The characteristic distribution of the mountain ranges has already been described. The chief peaks of the great snowy range in order from west to east are—Dhaulagiri (26,826 feet), two unnamed summits north-west of Kathmandu (26,069 and 25,818 feet), Gosainthan (26,305 feet), Mount Everest (29,002 feet), and Kanchinjunga (27,315 feet). To the west of Dhaulagiri the highest peaks are below 23,000 feet.

Dhaulagiri is the culminating point of the range between the feeders of the Gogra and those of the Gandak, and from its southern flank proceed the upper waters of the Rapti. Gosainthan is the highest peak of that which separates the basins of the Gandak and the Kosi, and Mount Everest rises between the Bhotiakosi and the Kosi, the former a tributary of the latter, which drains an extensive area of the Tibetan table-land north of the great snowy range. Kanchinjunga, on the frontier of Nepal and Sikkim, is on the range that divides the Kosi from the Teesta. The lower courses of these great rivers have been already noticed under the North-West Provinces and Bengal.

Towns.—All the towns of any importance are clustered in the Kathmandu valley. The principal of them are—Kathmandu, the present capital (about 50,000); Patan (60,000), the capital of the former Newar rulers, who were conquered by the Górkhas in 1768, and still the largest city; and Bhatgaon (50,000).

Population.—The inhabitants of Nepal are estimated at about 2 millions, which would give about 36 to the square mile on an average. Those of the northern mountains are Tibetans of Mongol race. Those of the southern mountains are partly Mongol, partly Indian, but for the most part much mixed; and those of the Terái are various tribes of Indian aboriginals. The ruling race, the Górkhas, are the descendants of Brahmans and Rájputs driven out of India by the Muhammadan invaders, but now largely mixed with Mongol blood. They are a small, active, warlike race, and some of the best regiments of the Indian native army are entirely recruited from them. The Newars of the central part of Nepal are chiefly cultivators or traders. The language of the Górkhas, called Parbhatiya (hill language), is Aryan, and they are Hindu by religion. The Bhotiyas, Newars, and some other tribes are Buddhists, but much Hinduised.

Productions.—There is a considerable export trade from Nepal in blue vitriol, the tough soft paper made from the paper laurel, cardamoms, elephants, hides, horns, and wax, which are the produce of the outer hills and the Terái; and also in borax, musk, yaks' tails, rhubarb, and ponies, which come from the mountains north of the snowy range and partly from Tibet beyond the frontier.

THE END

Printed by R. & R. Clark, *Edinburgh.*